Hey 'Uncle' Mike

Hope you enjoy the read,

Theo

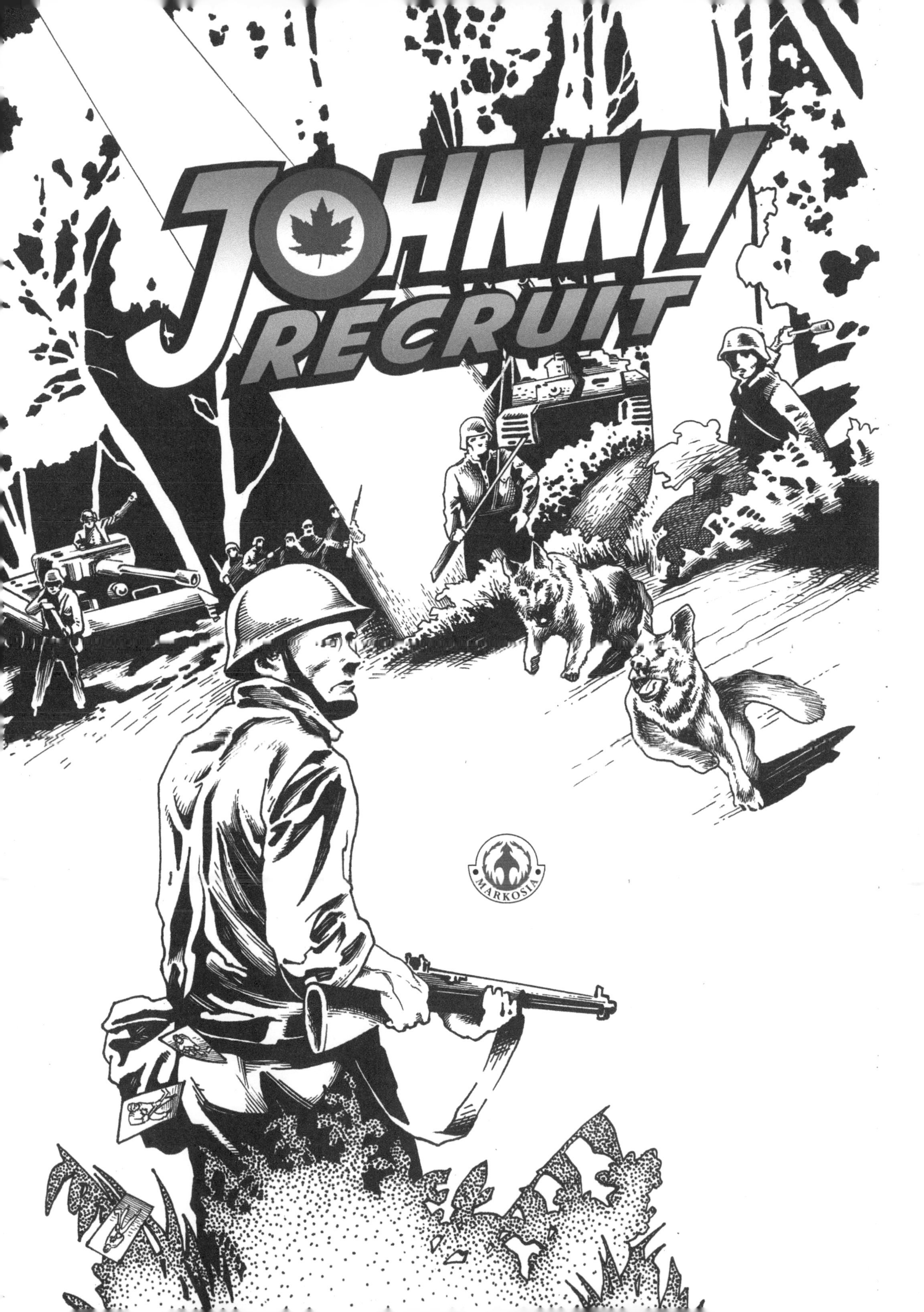
JOHNNY
RECRUIT
MARKOSIA

FOR MARKOSIA ENTERPRISES LTD

HARRY MARKOS
Publisher &
Managing Partner

GM JORDAN
Special Projects
Co-Ordinator

ANNIKA EADE
Media Manager

ANDY BRIGGS
Creative Consultant

MEIRION JONES
Marketing Director

IAN SHARMAN
Editor In Chief

 Published by Markosia Enterprises, PO BOX 3477, Barnet, Hertfordshire, EN5 9HN. FIRST PRINTING, May 2022. Harry Markos, Director.

ISBN 978-1-915387-04-2

www.markosia.com

JOHNNY RECRUIT

By Theo Behe & Thomas Muzzell

MARKOSIA

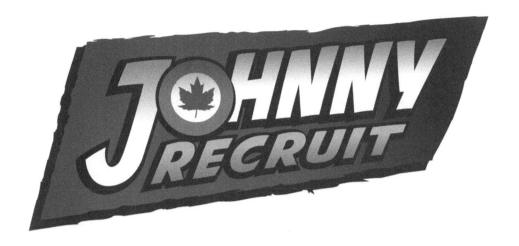

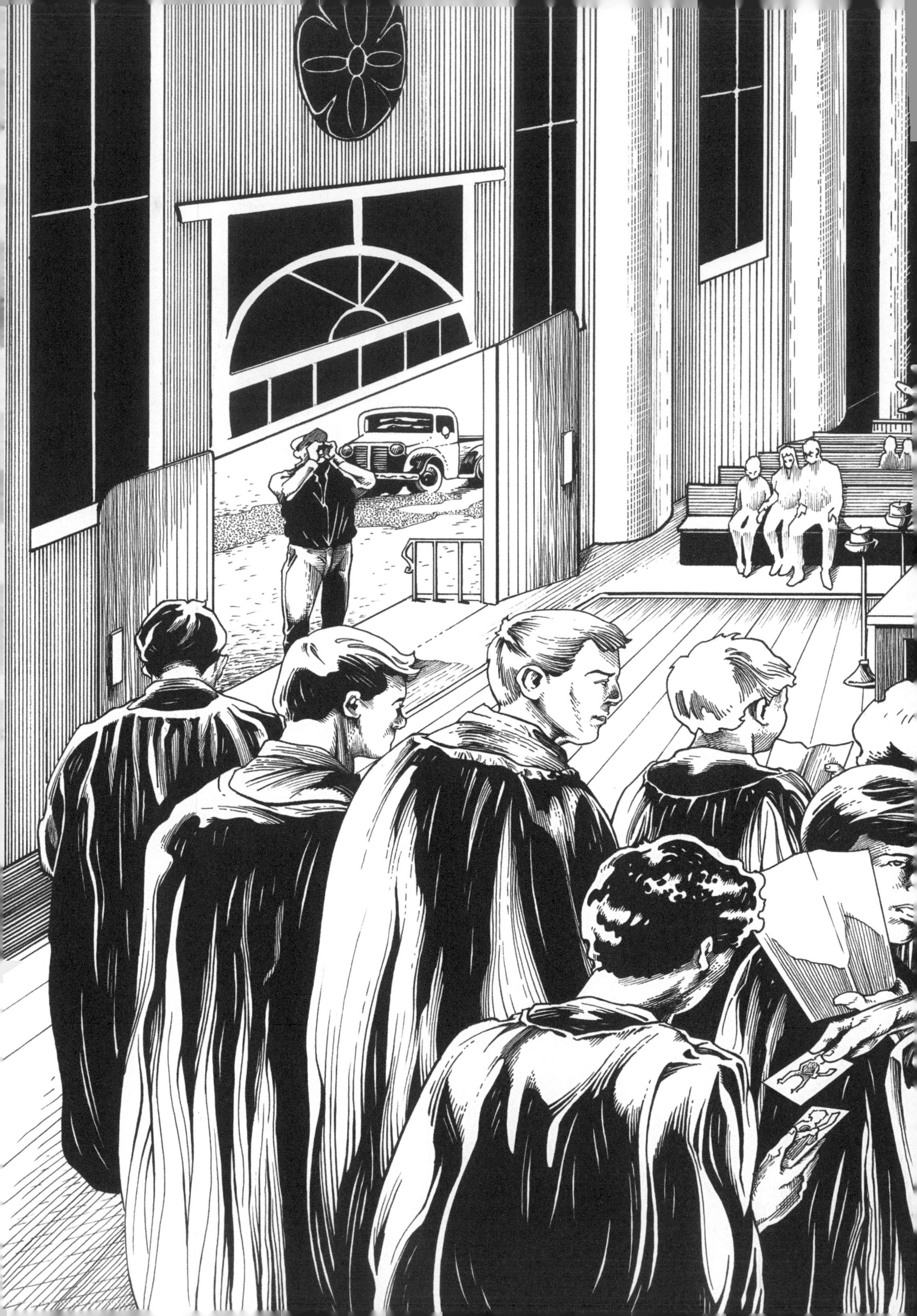

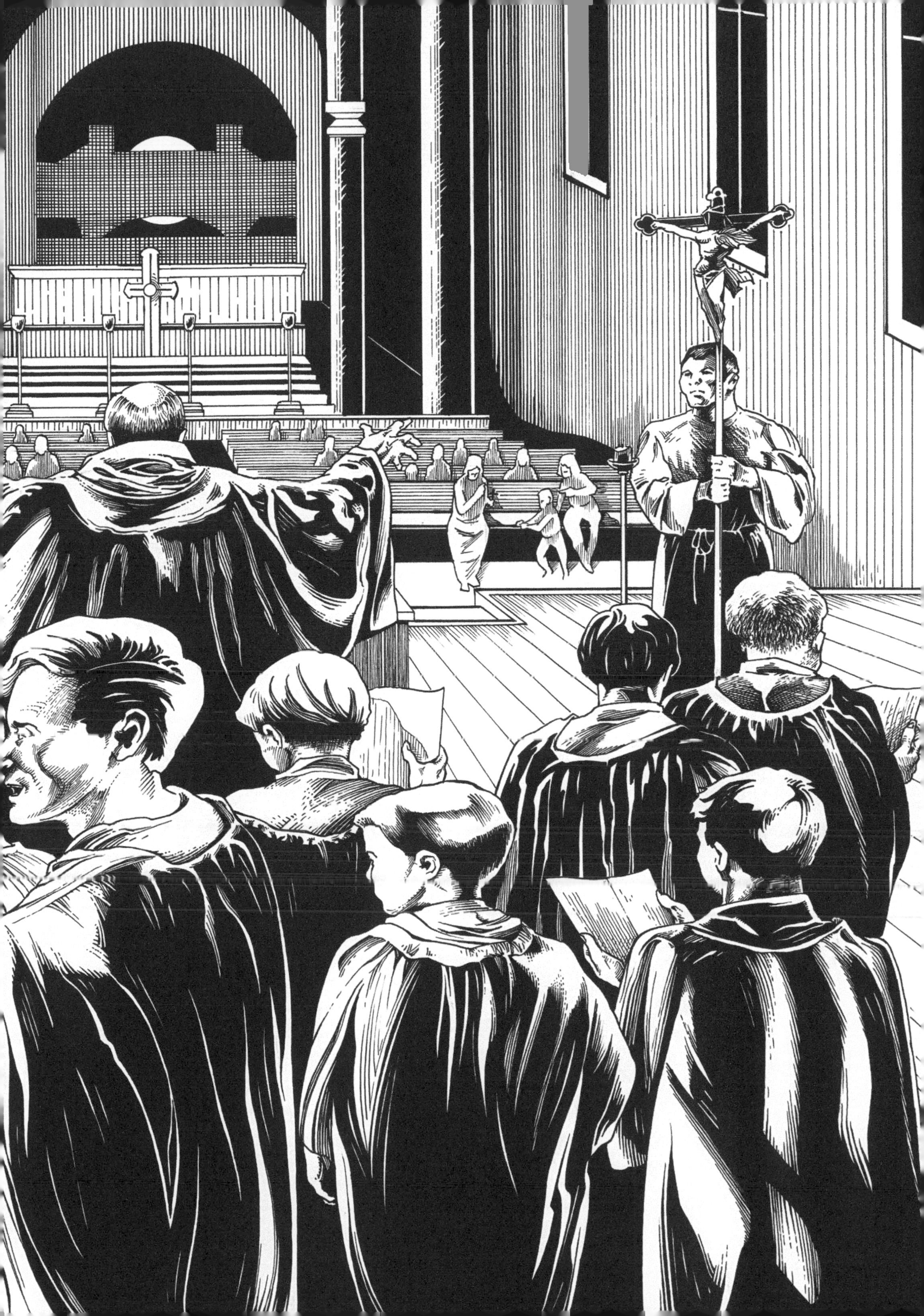

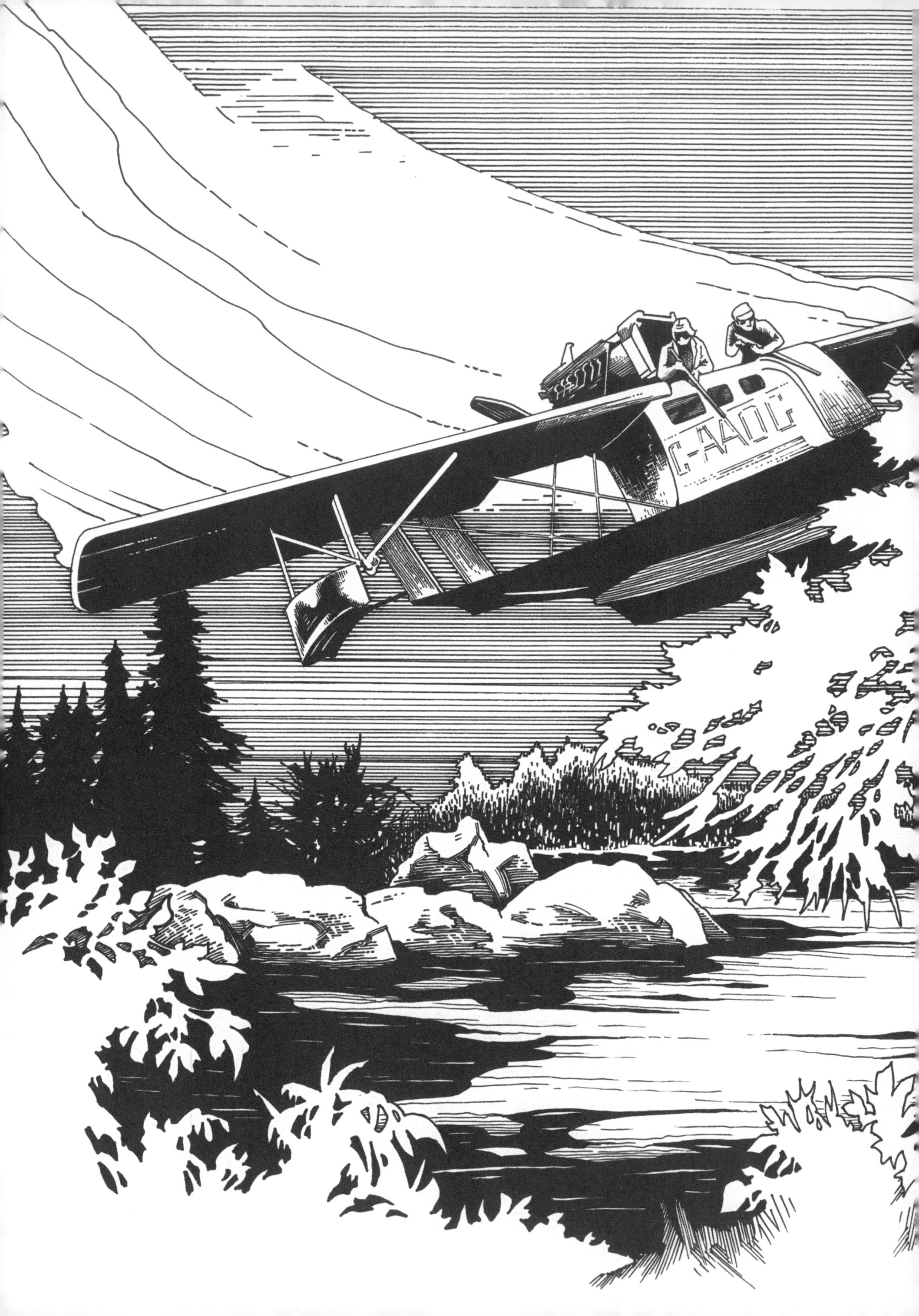

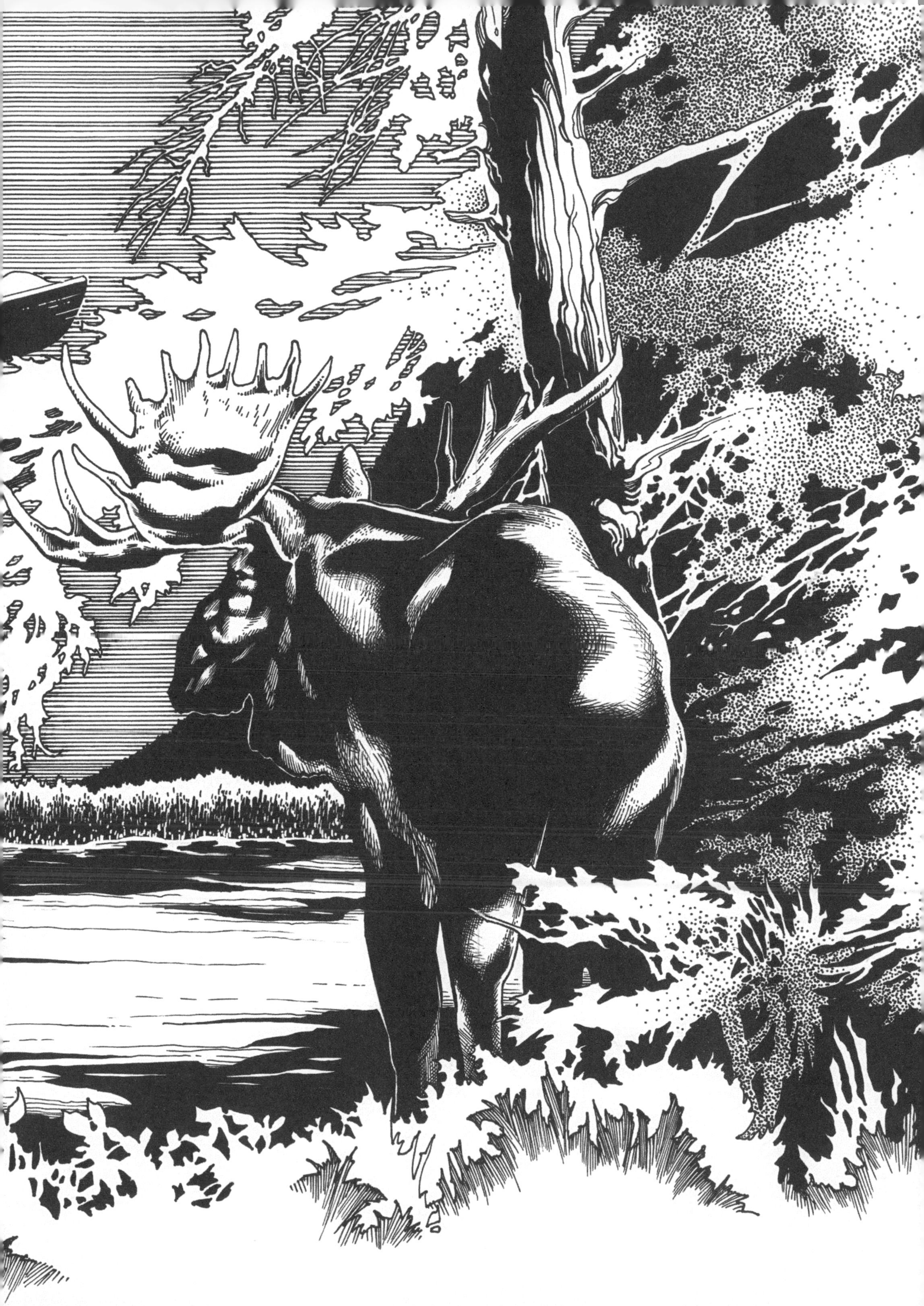

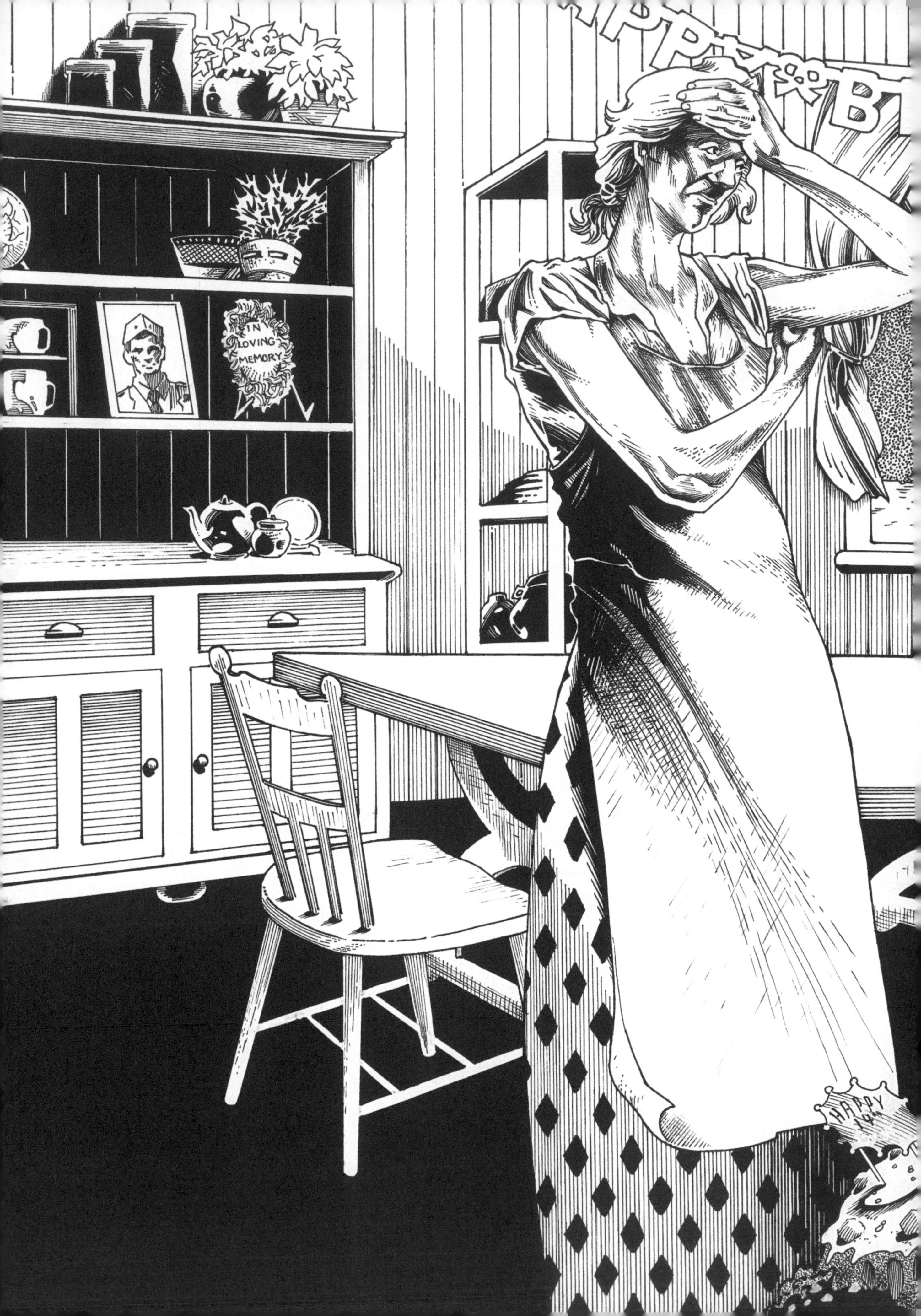
IN LOVING MEMORY
HAPPY 14th

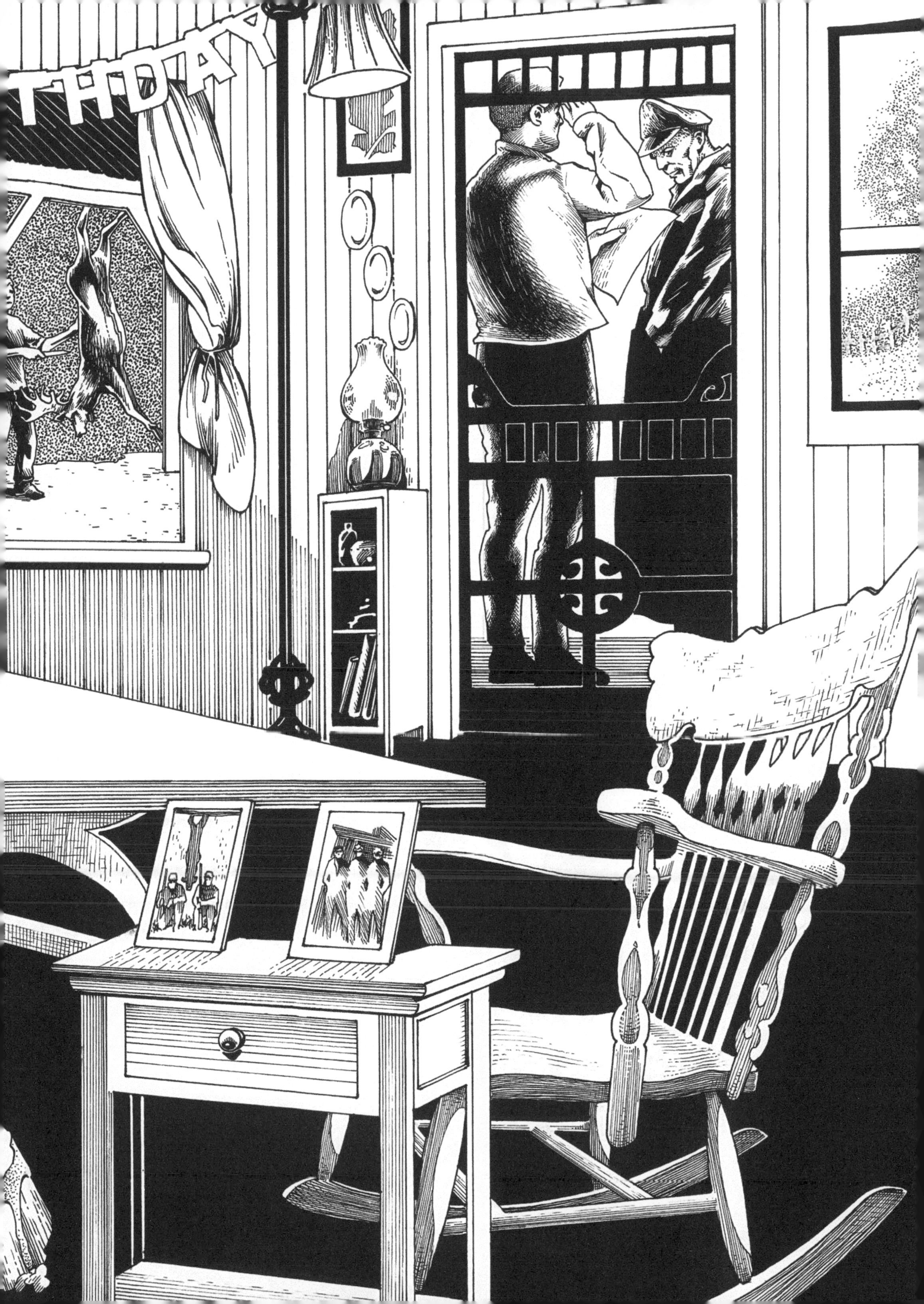
THDAY

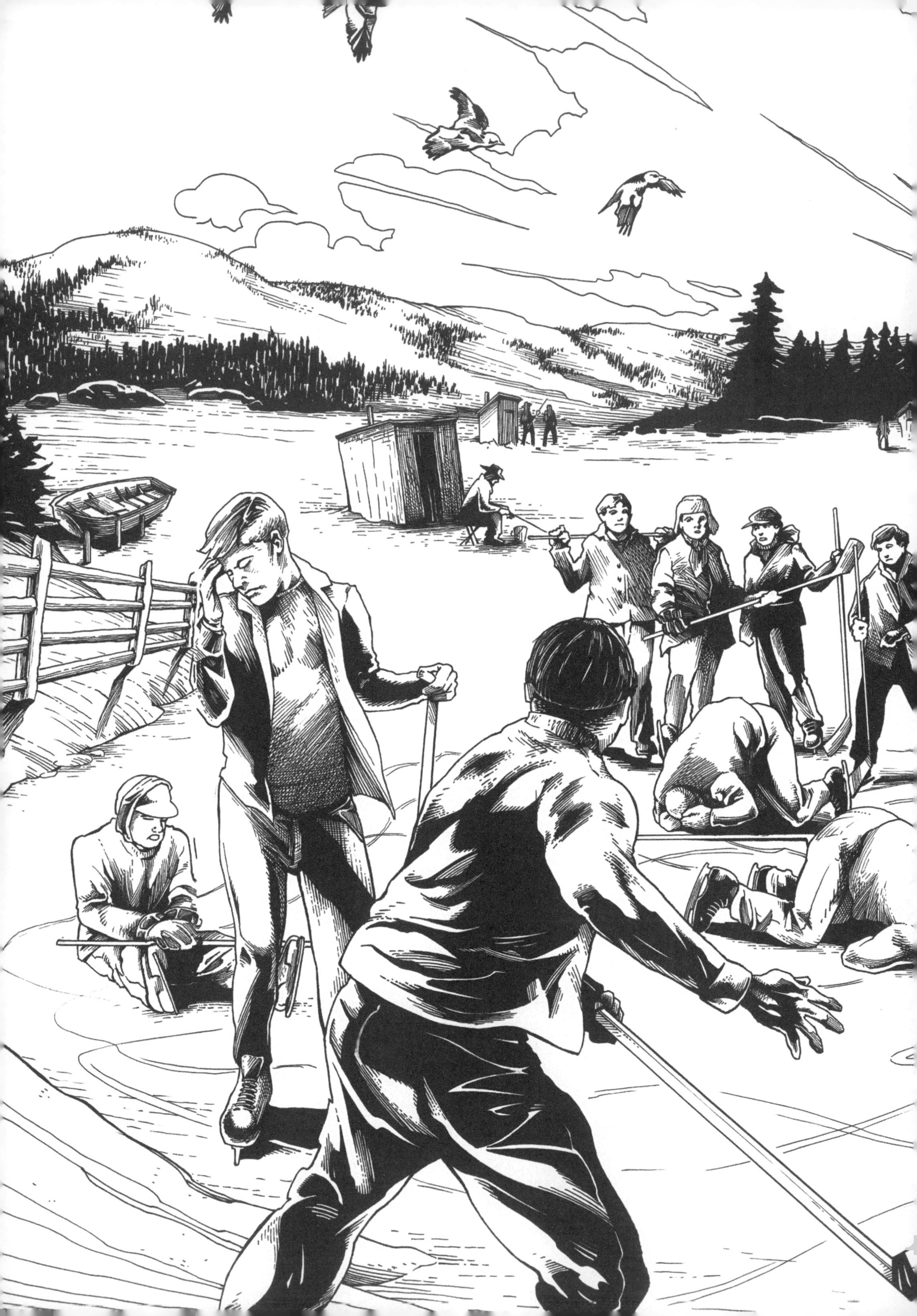

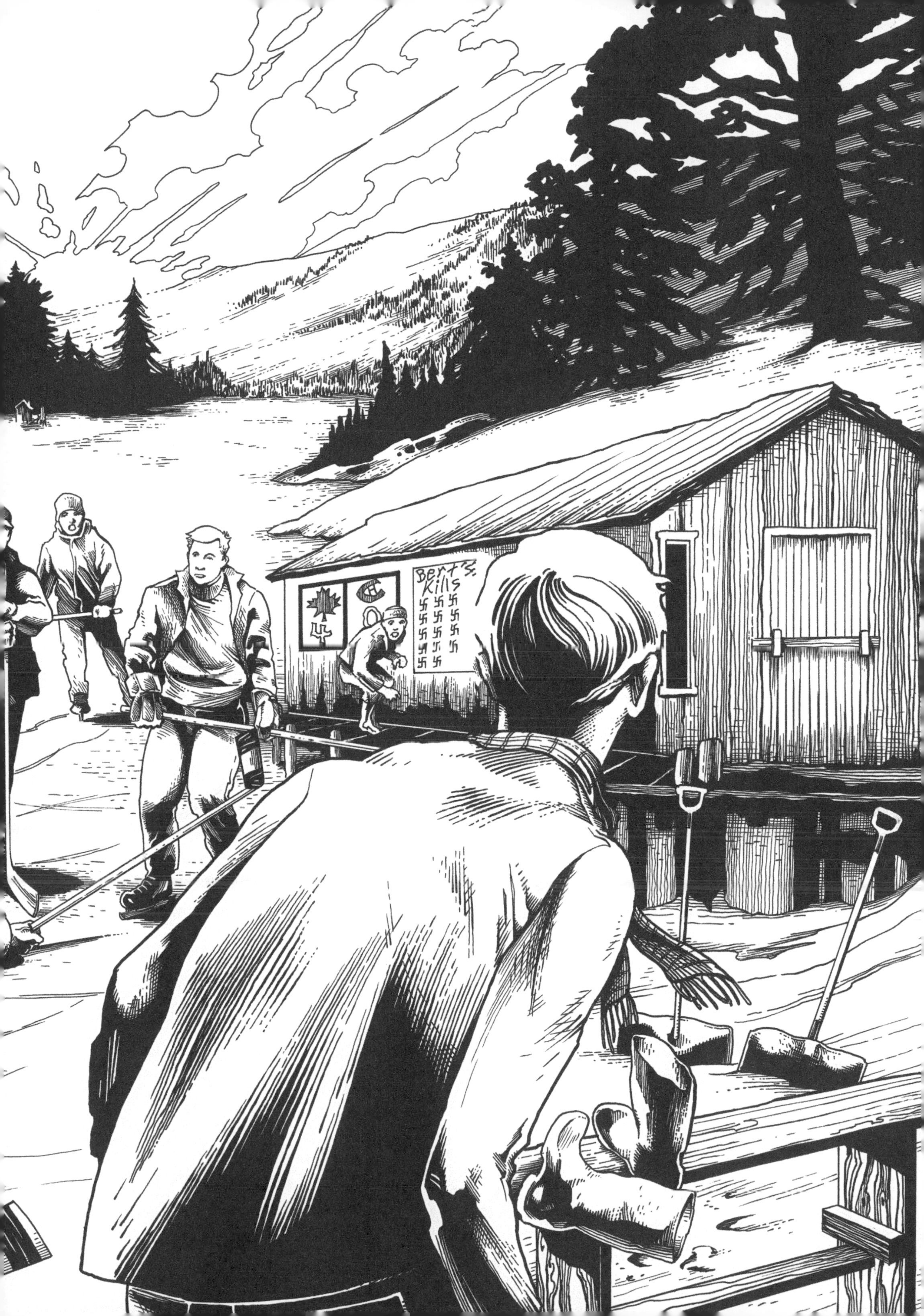
Bert's Kills

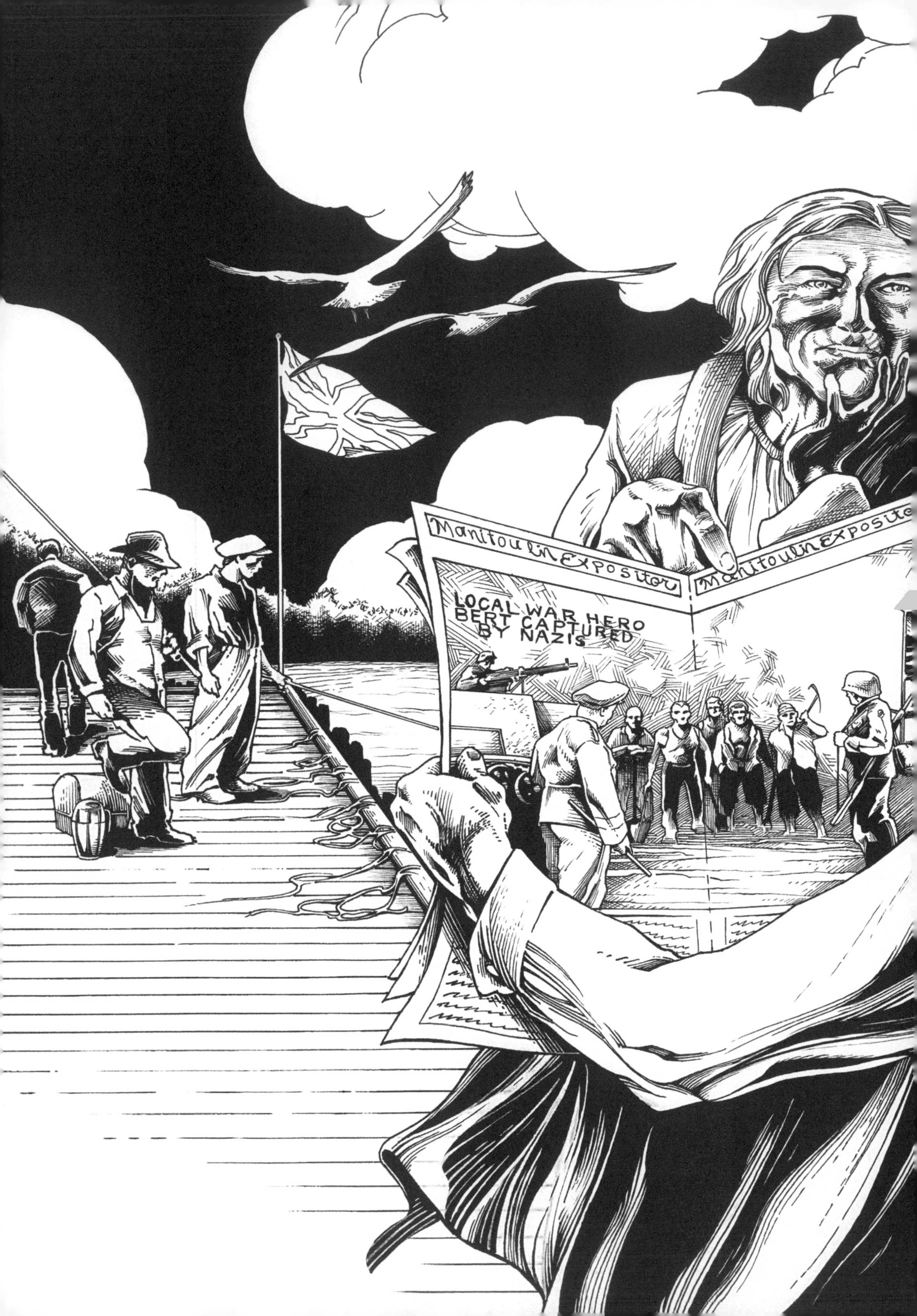
Manitoulin Expositor
Manitoulin Expositor
LOCAL WAR HERO
BERT CAPTURED
BY NAZIS

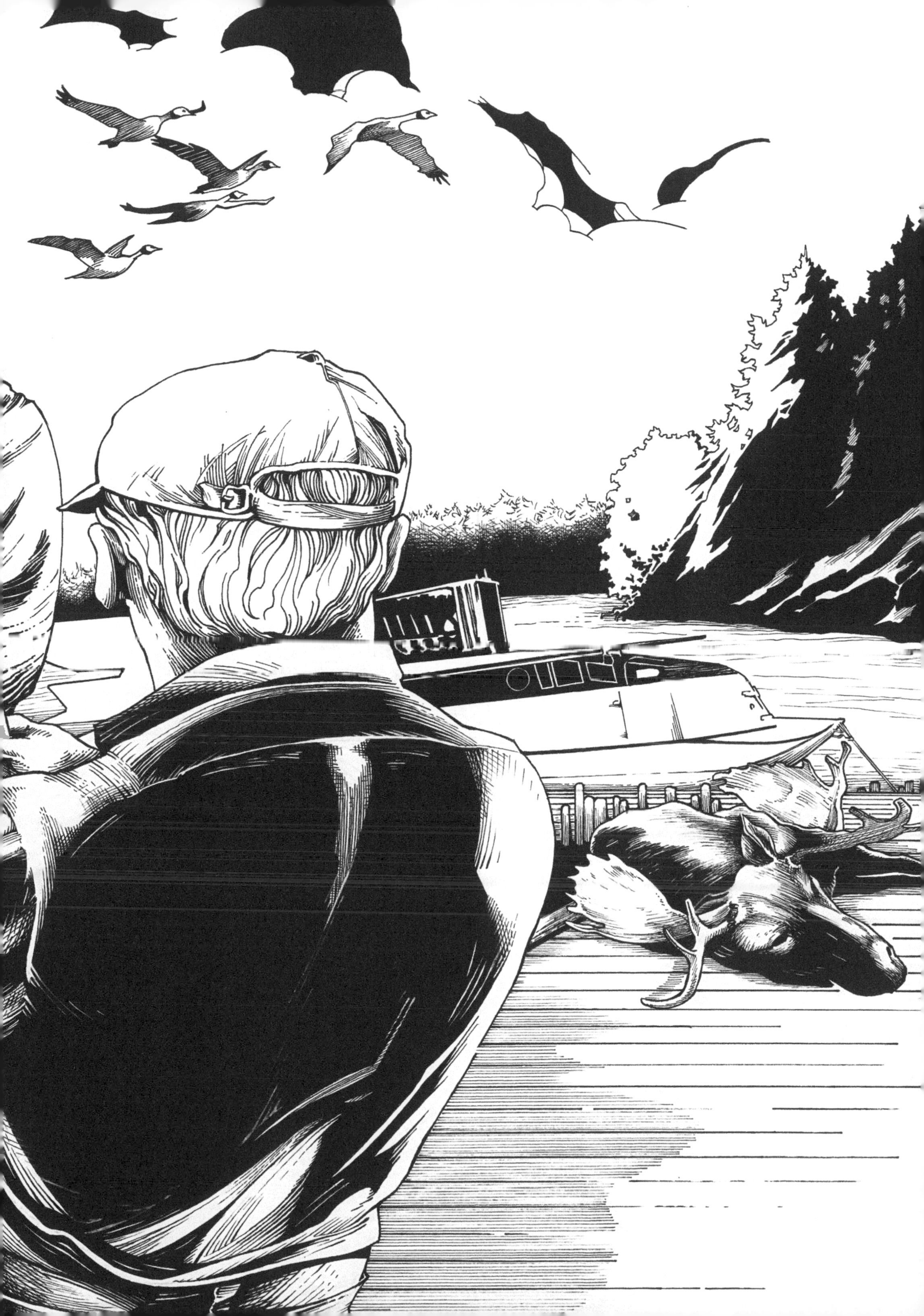

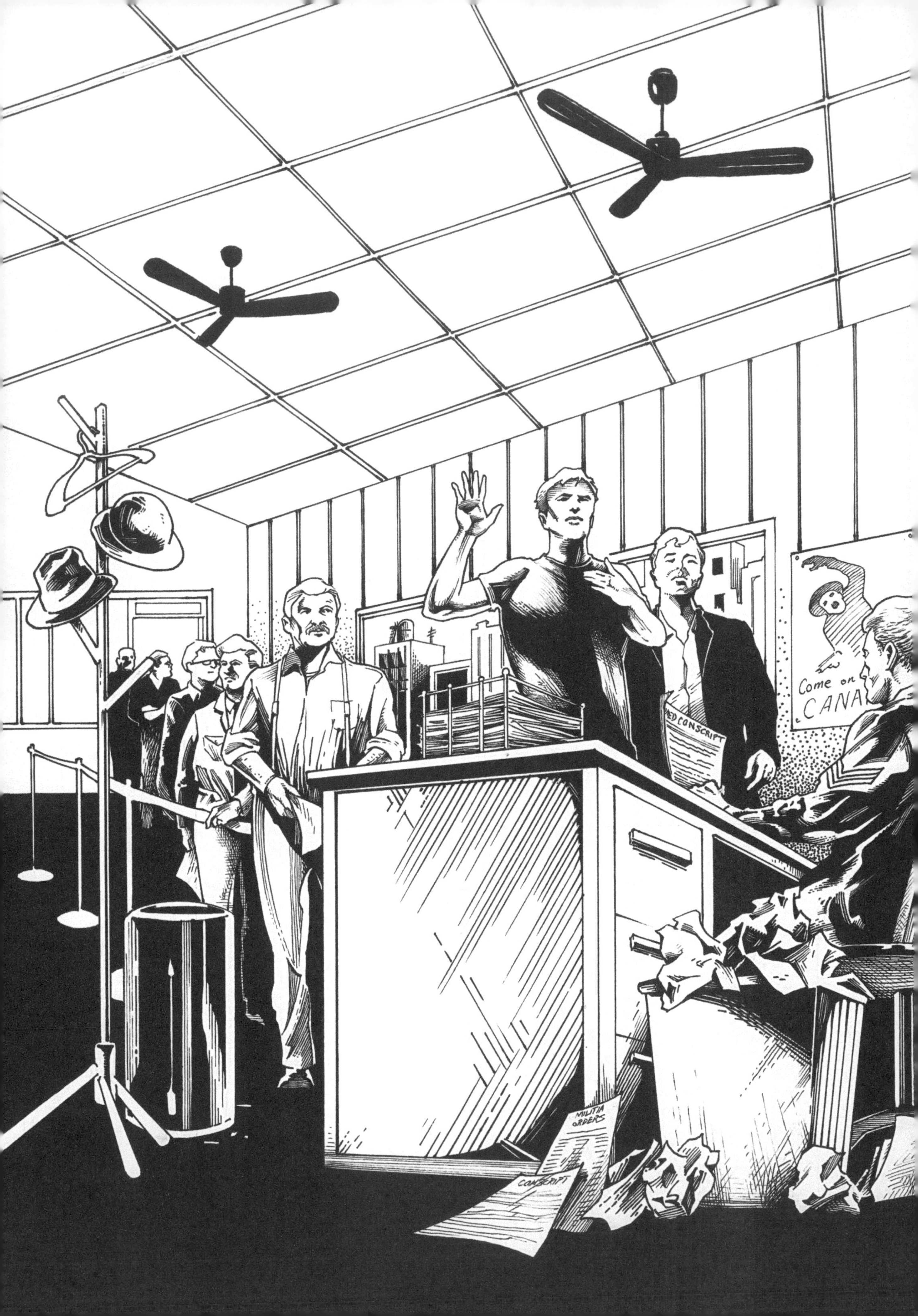
Come on
CANA
CONSCRIPT
MILITIA ORDERS
CONSCRIPT

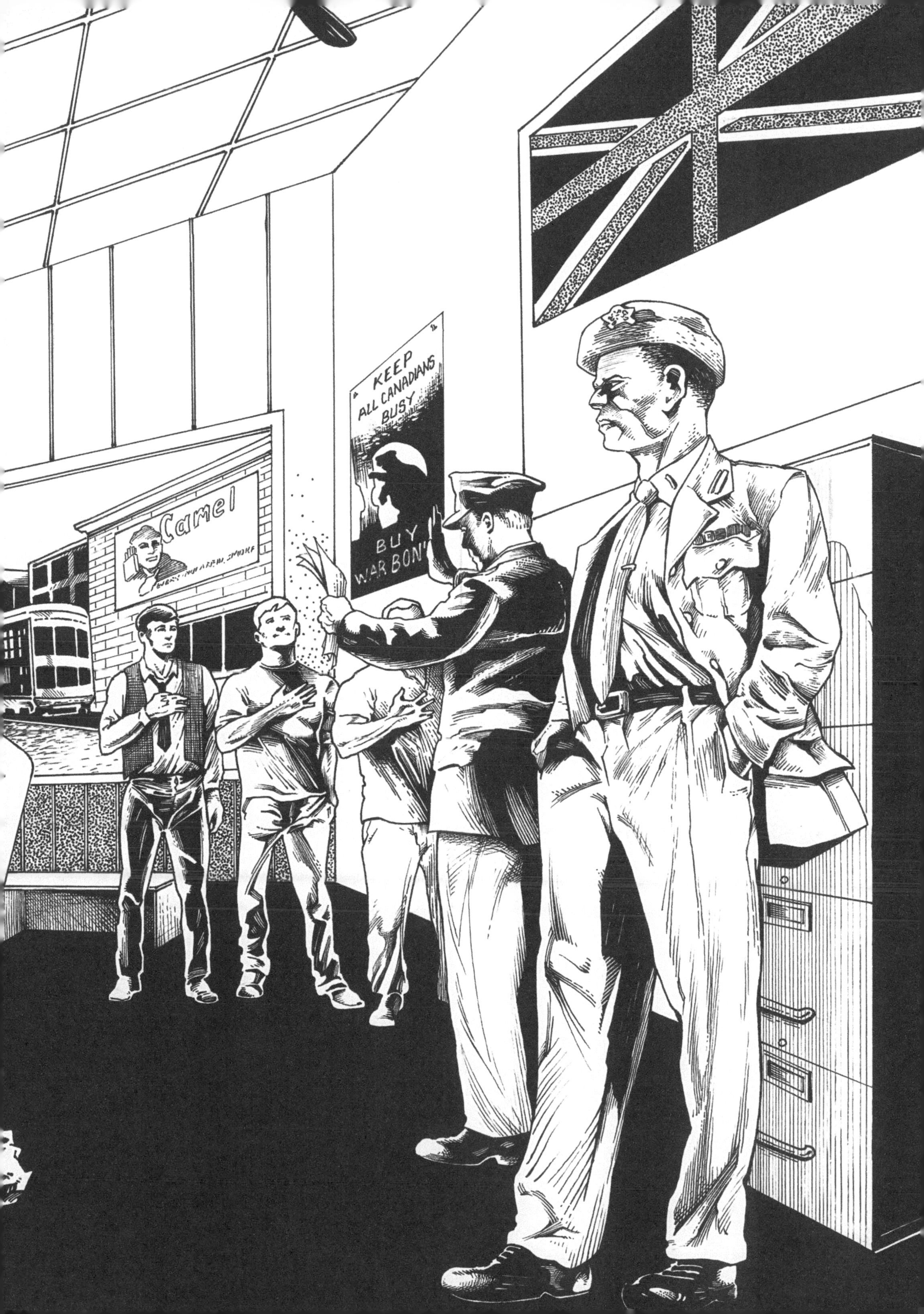
Camel
KEEP ALL CANADIANS BUSY
BUY
WAR BON

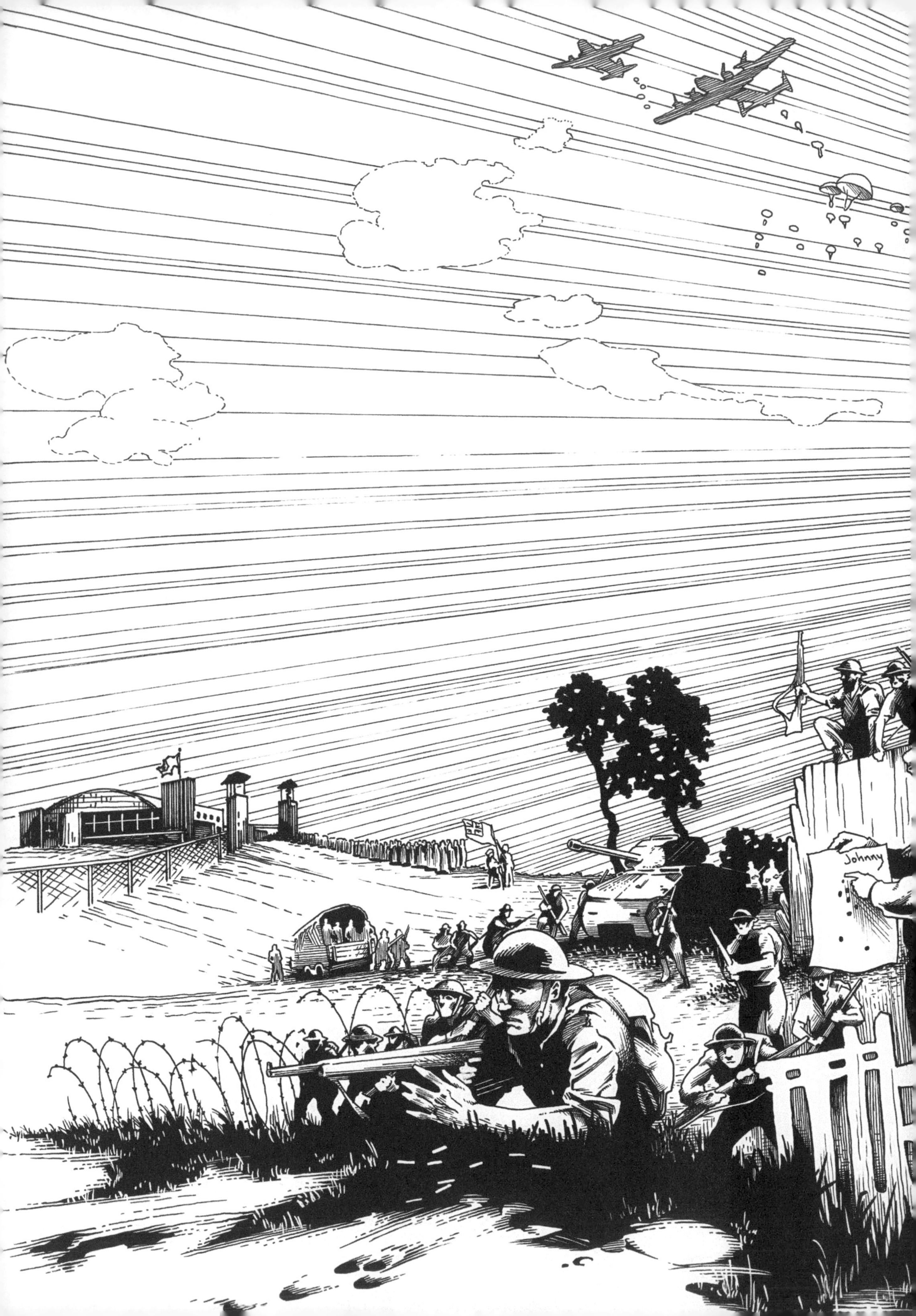
Johnny

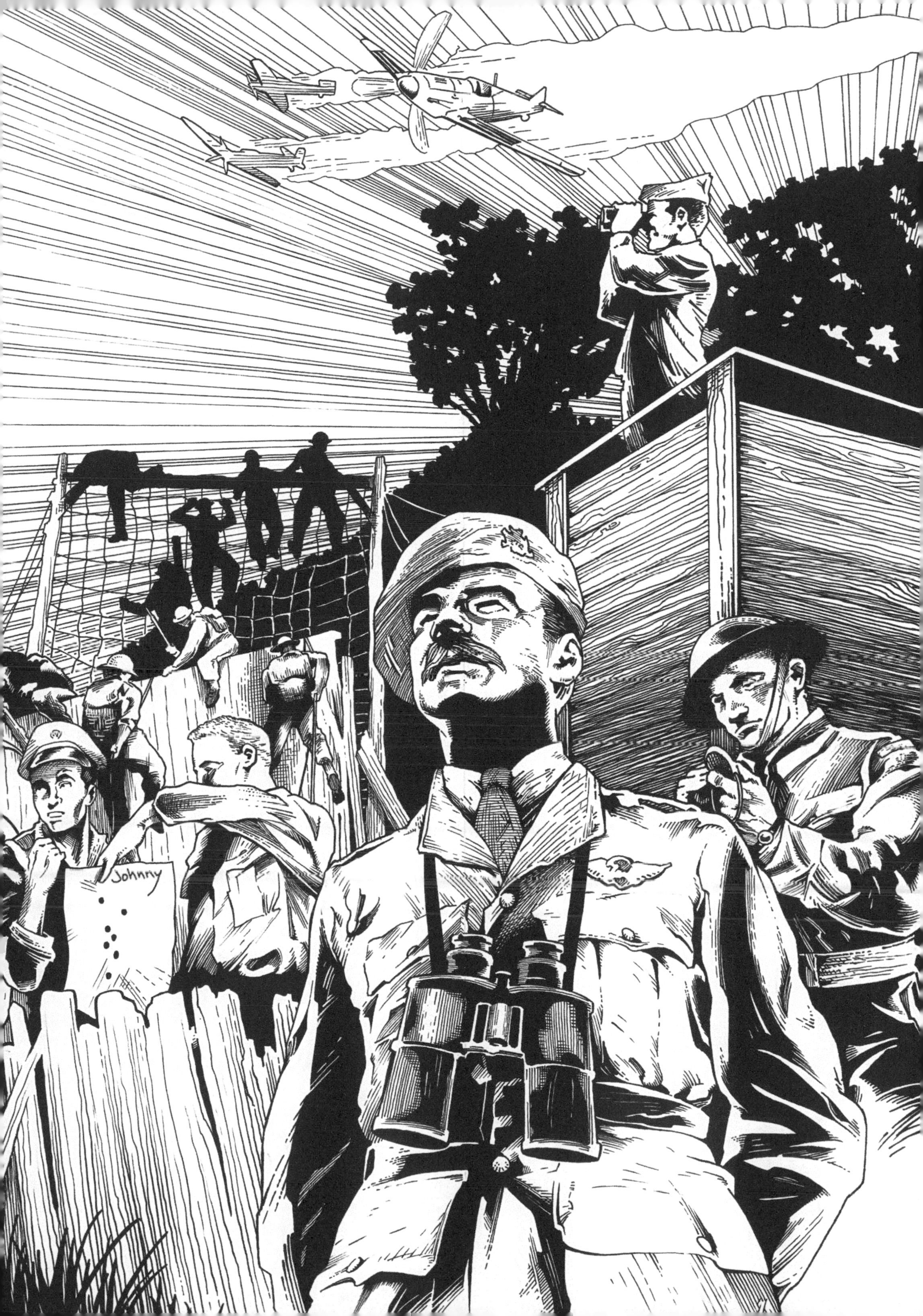
Johnny

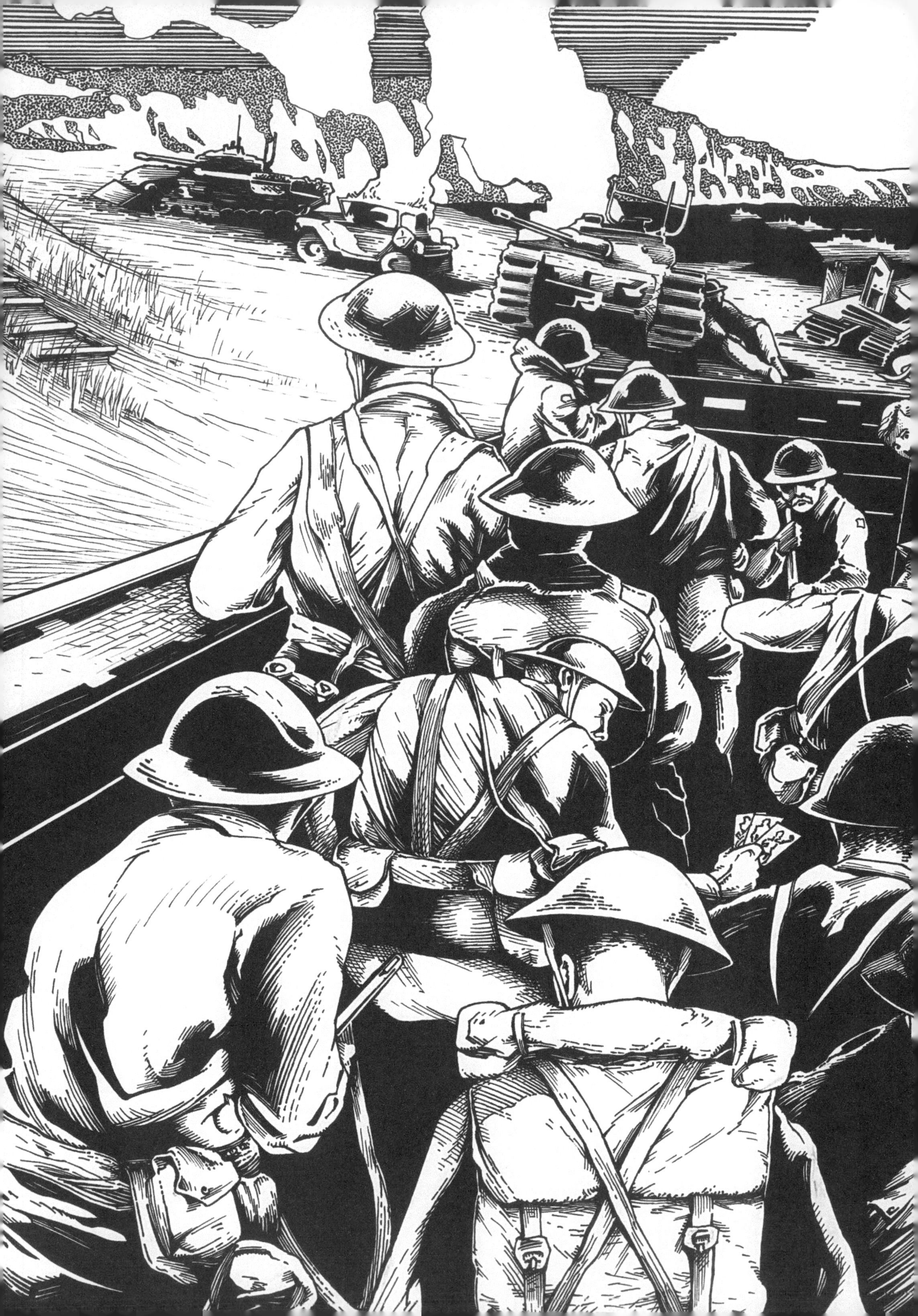

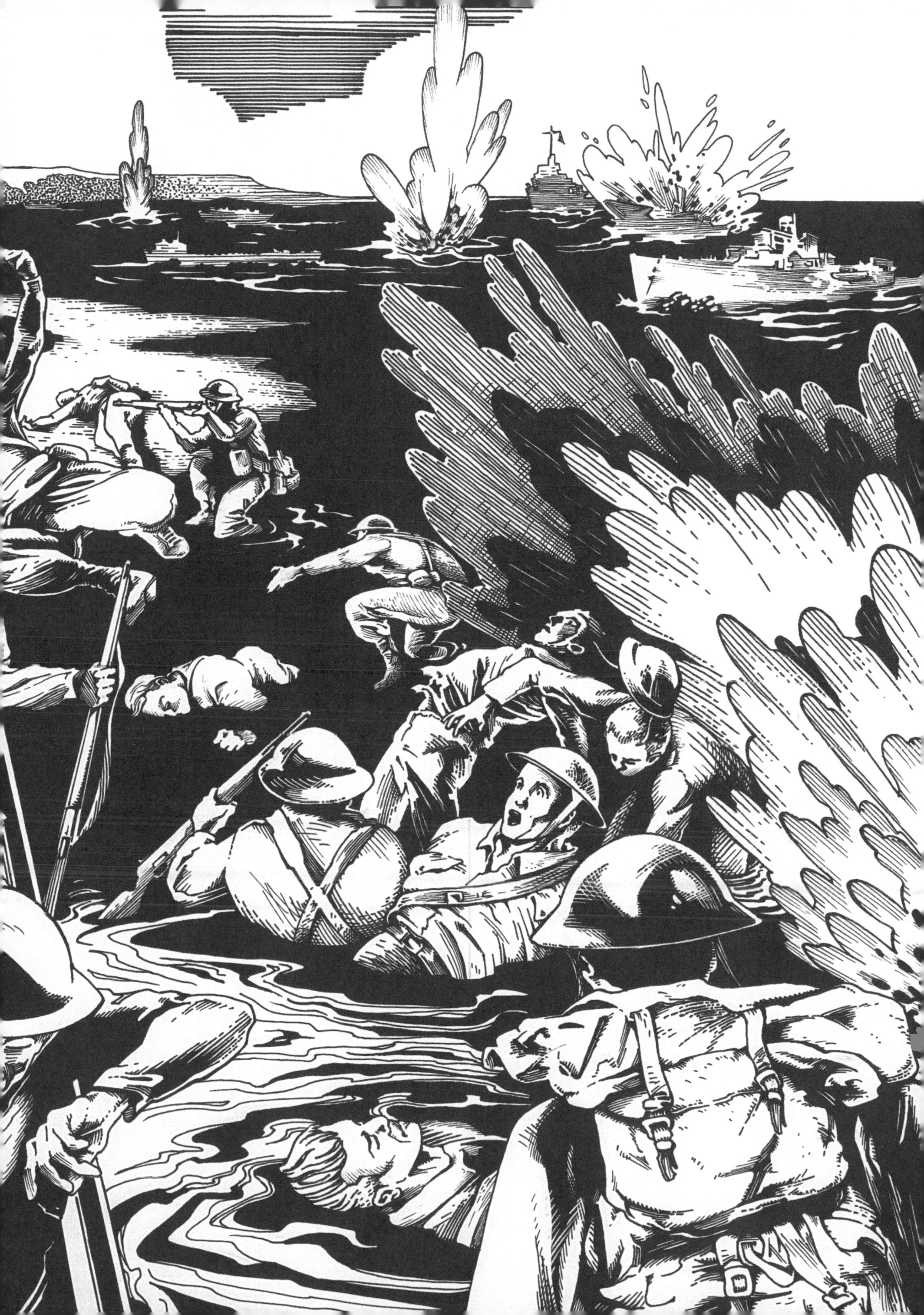

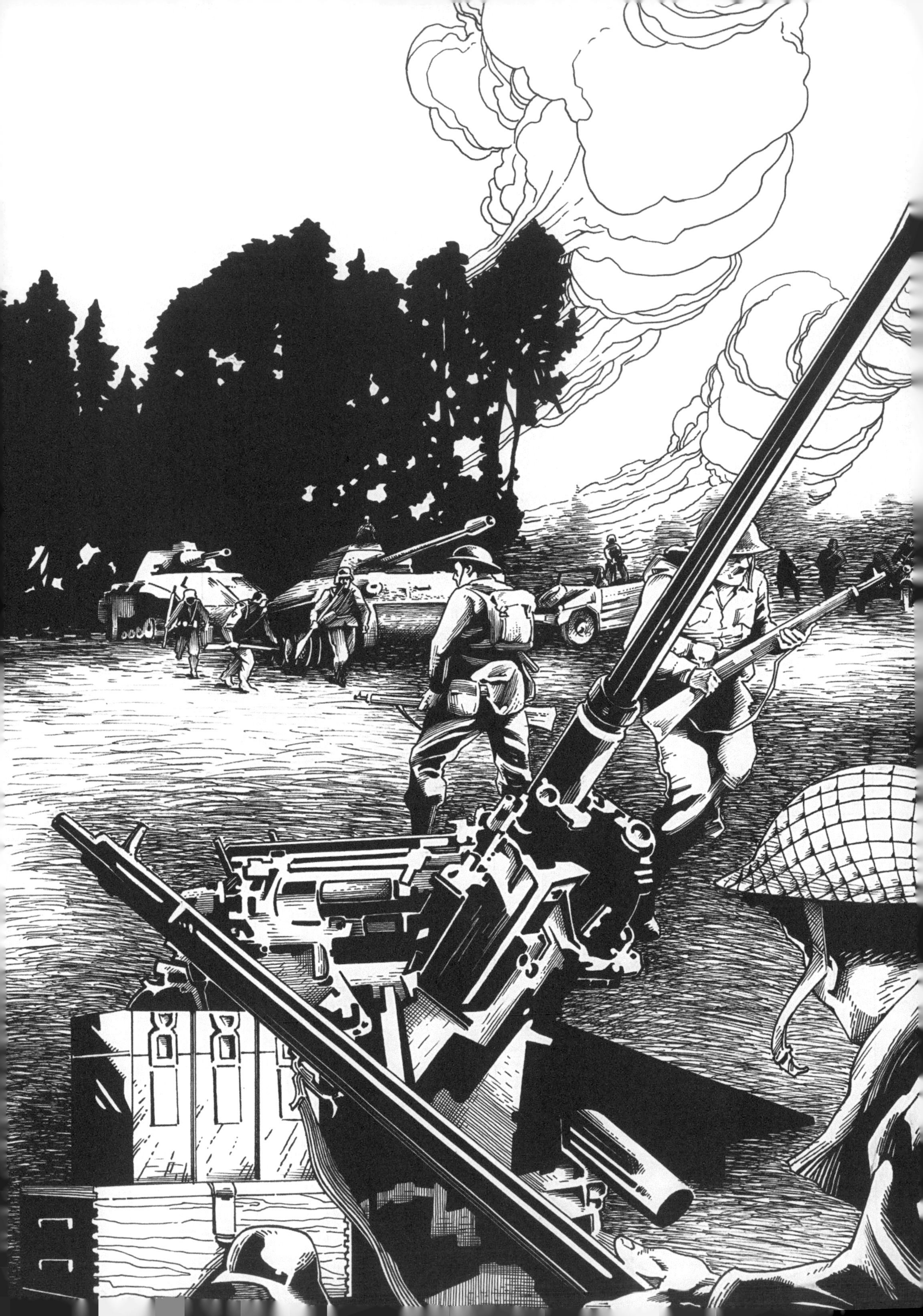

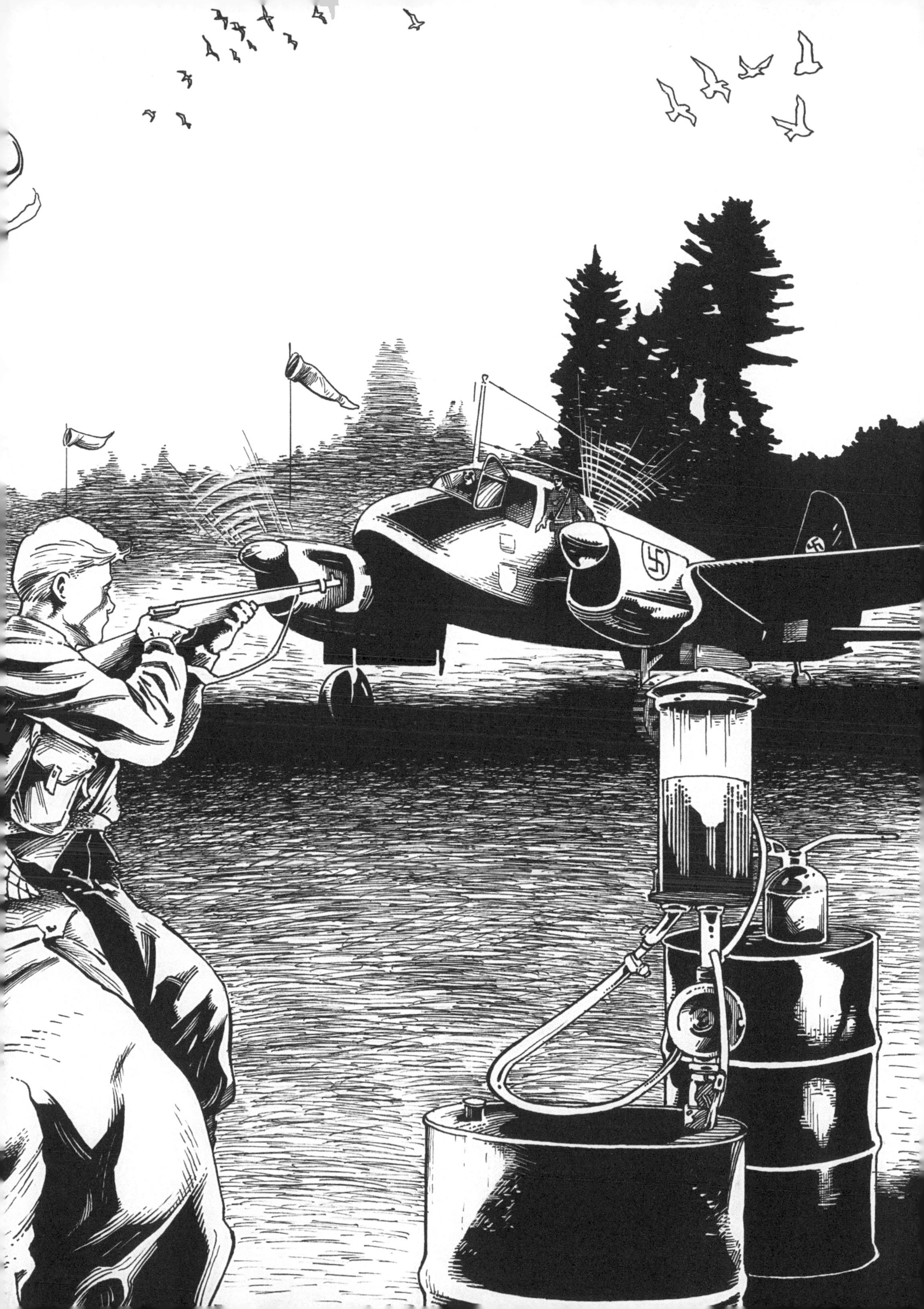

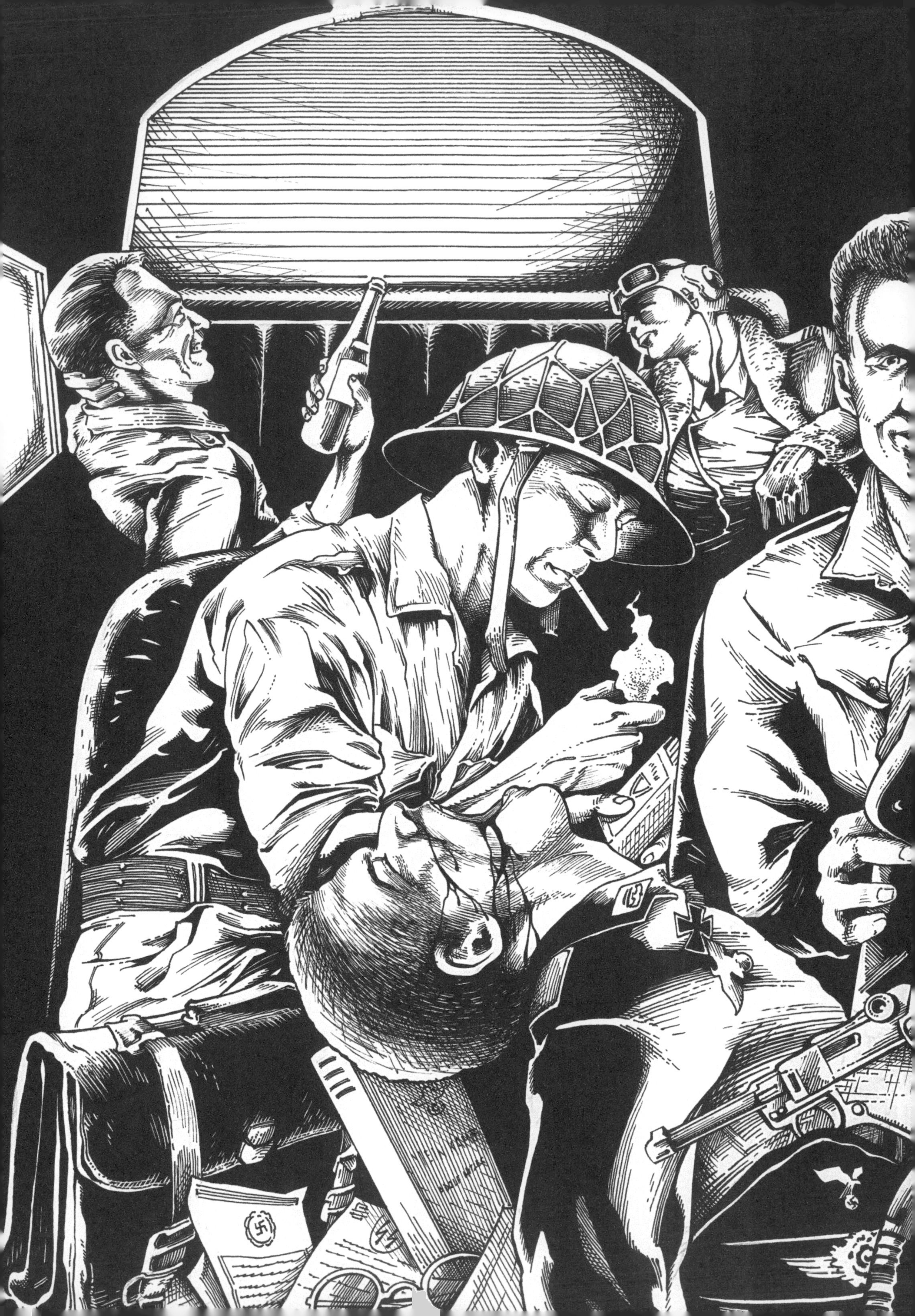

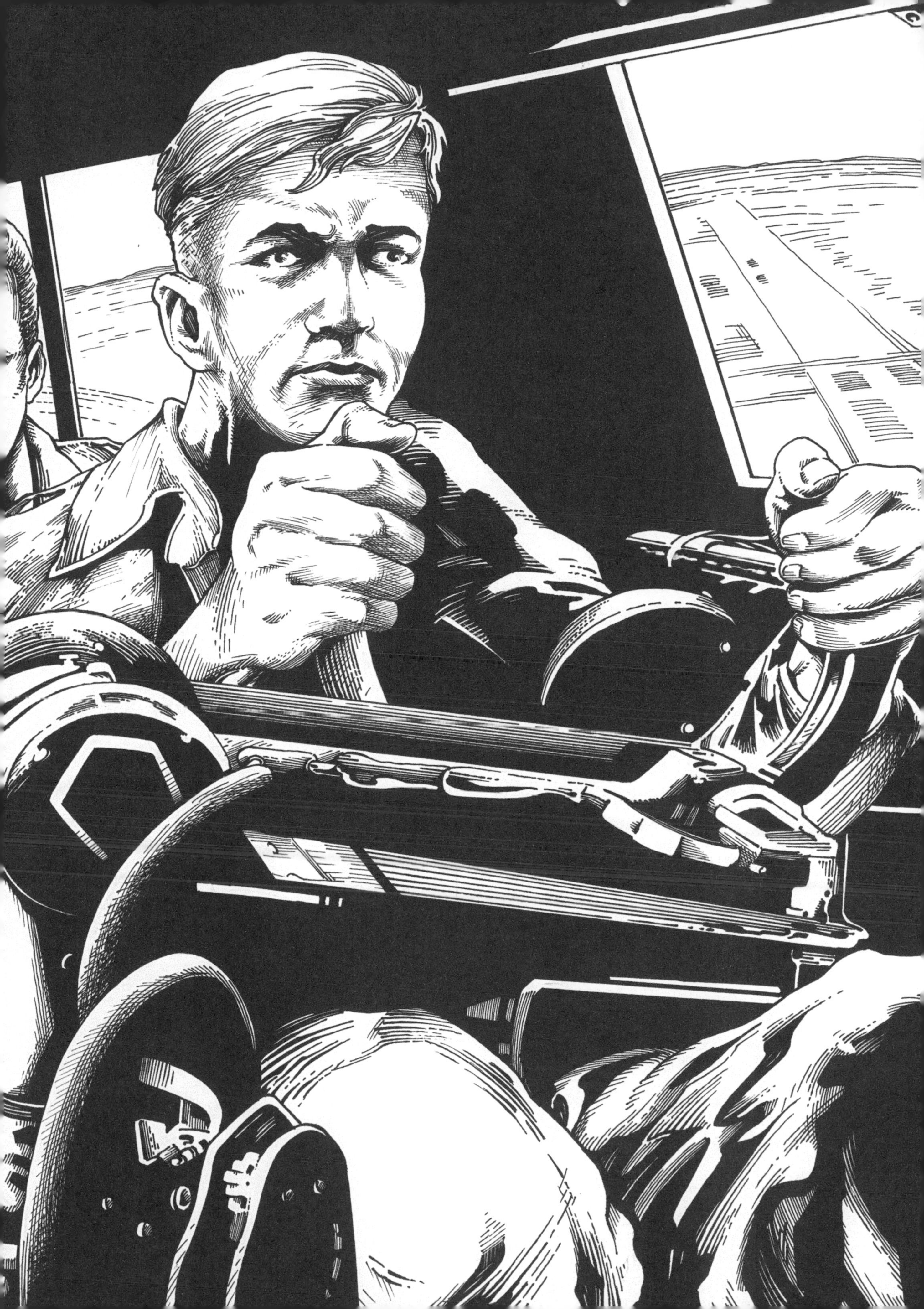

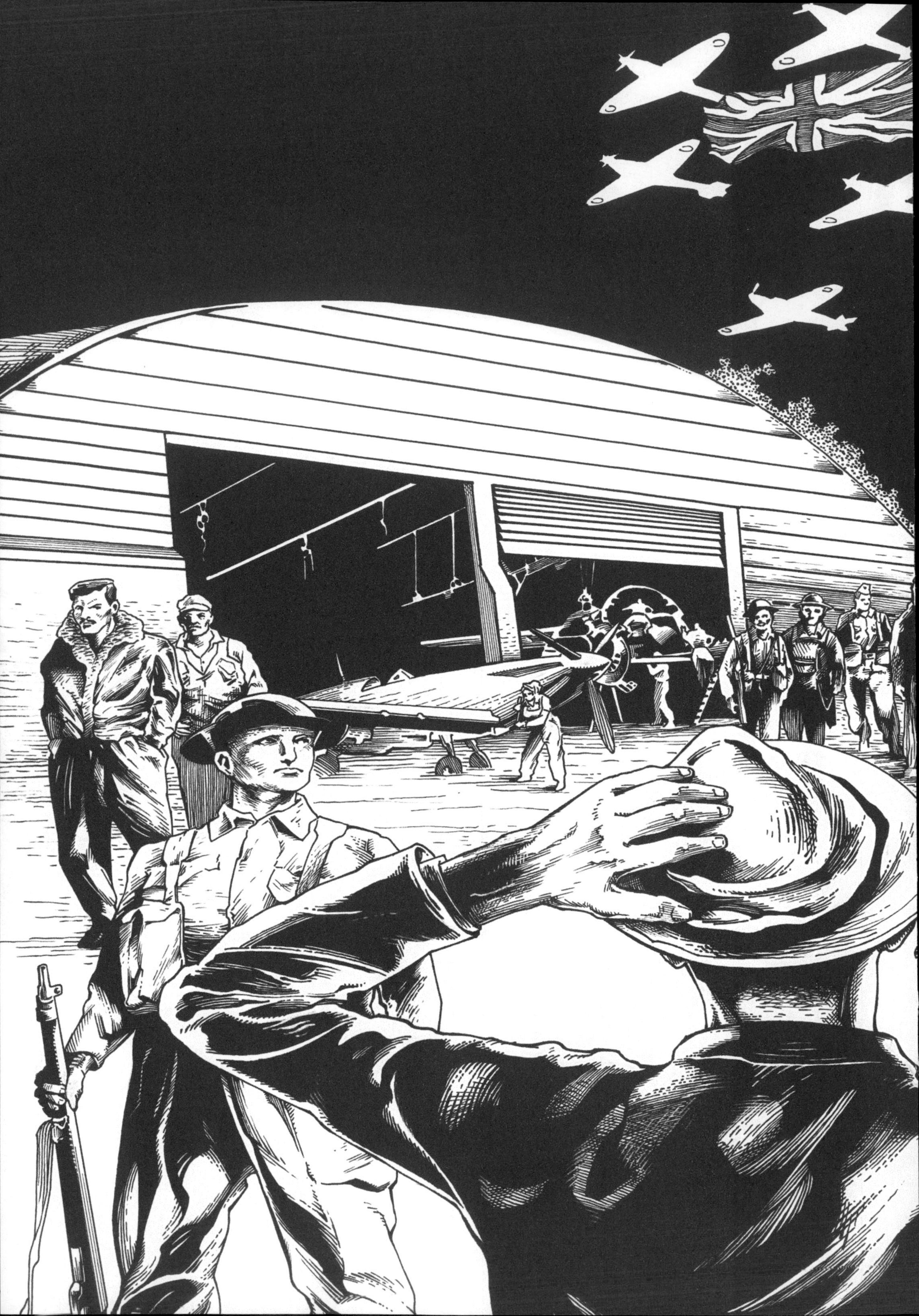

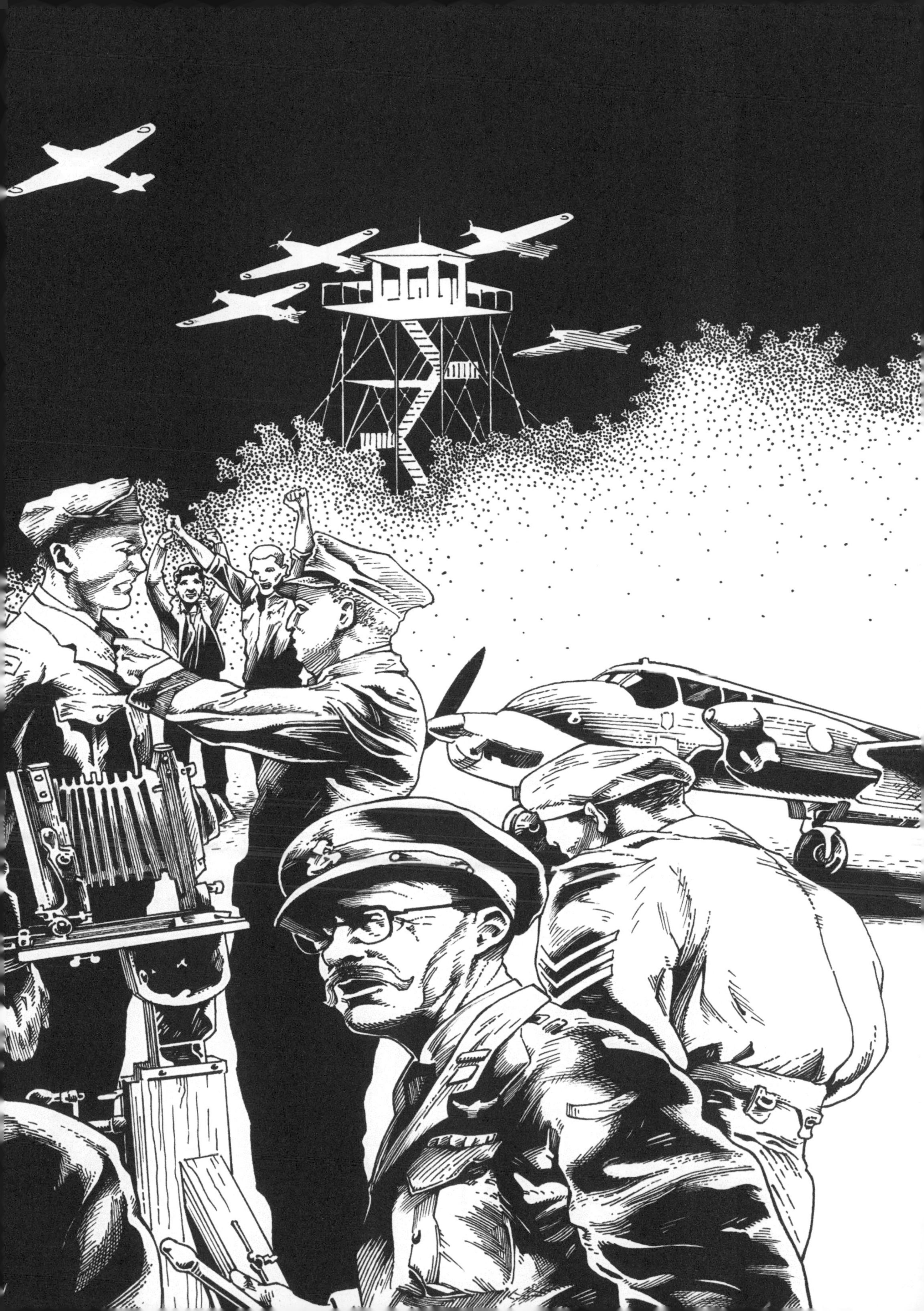

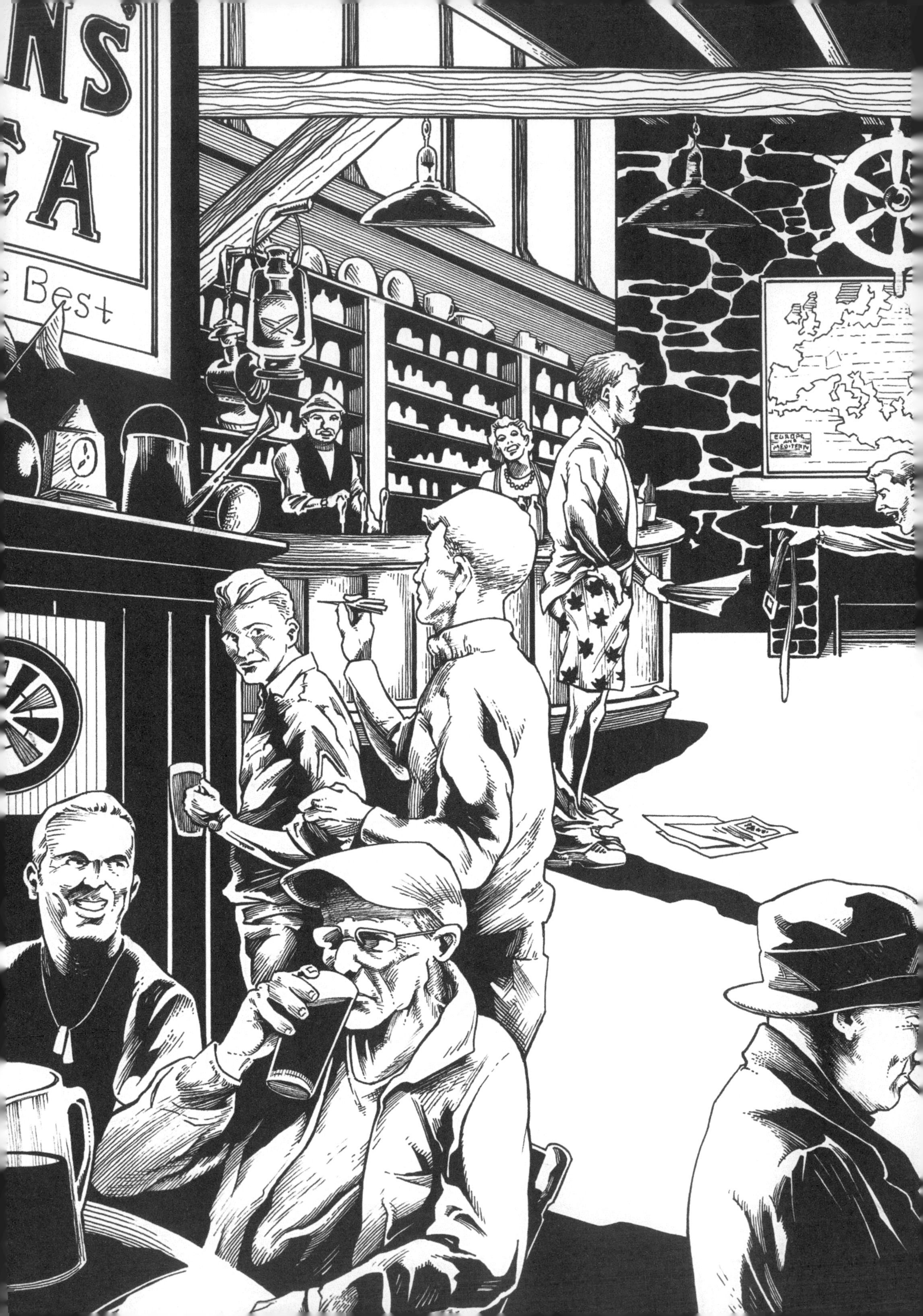

Best

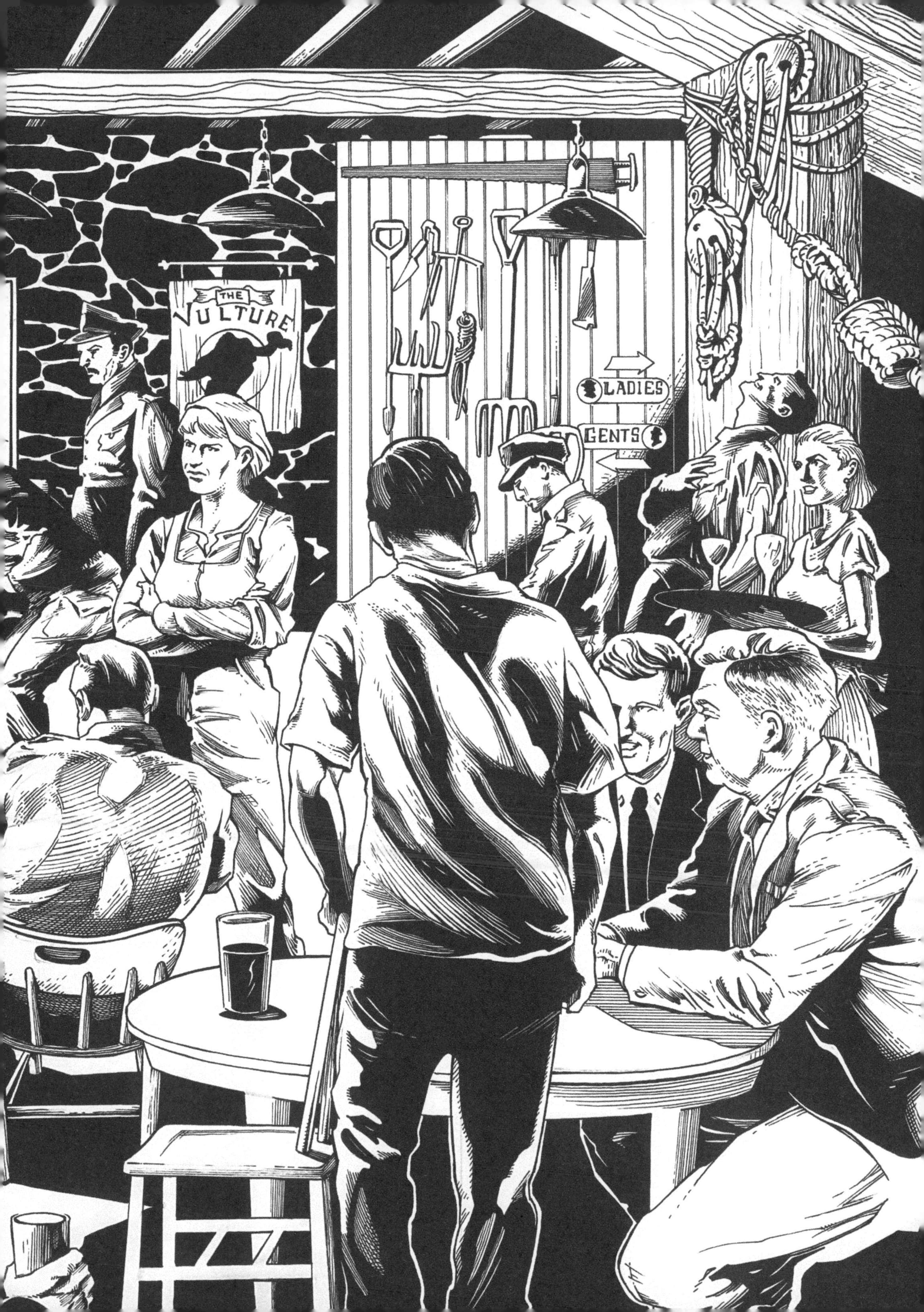
THE
VULTURE
LADIES
GENTS

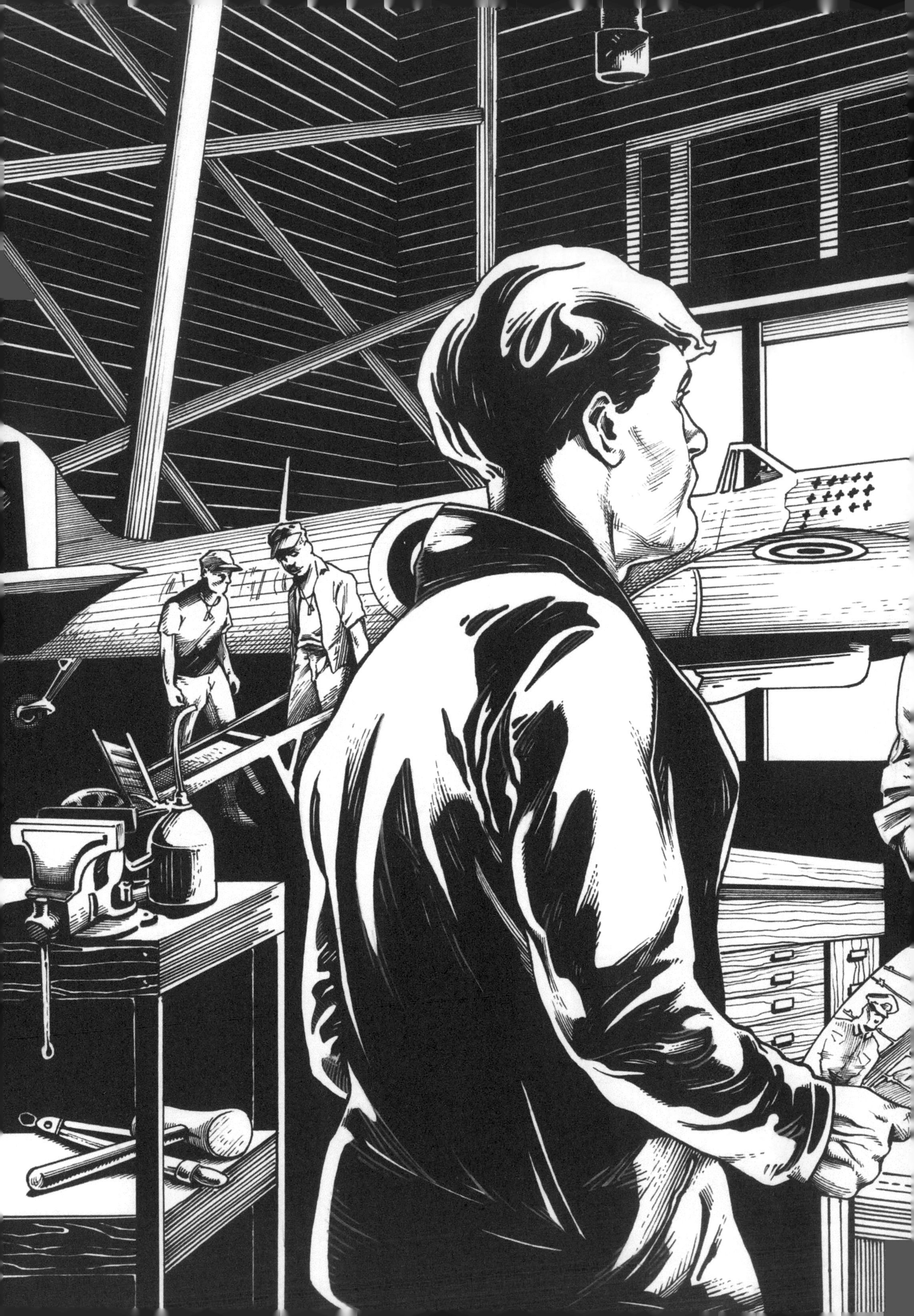

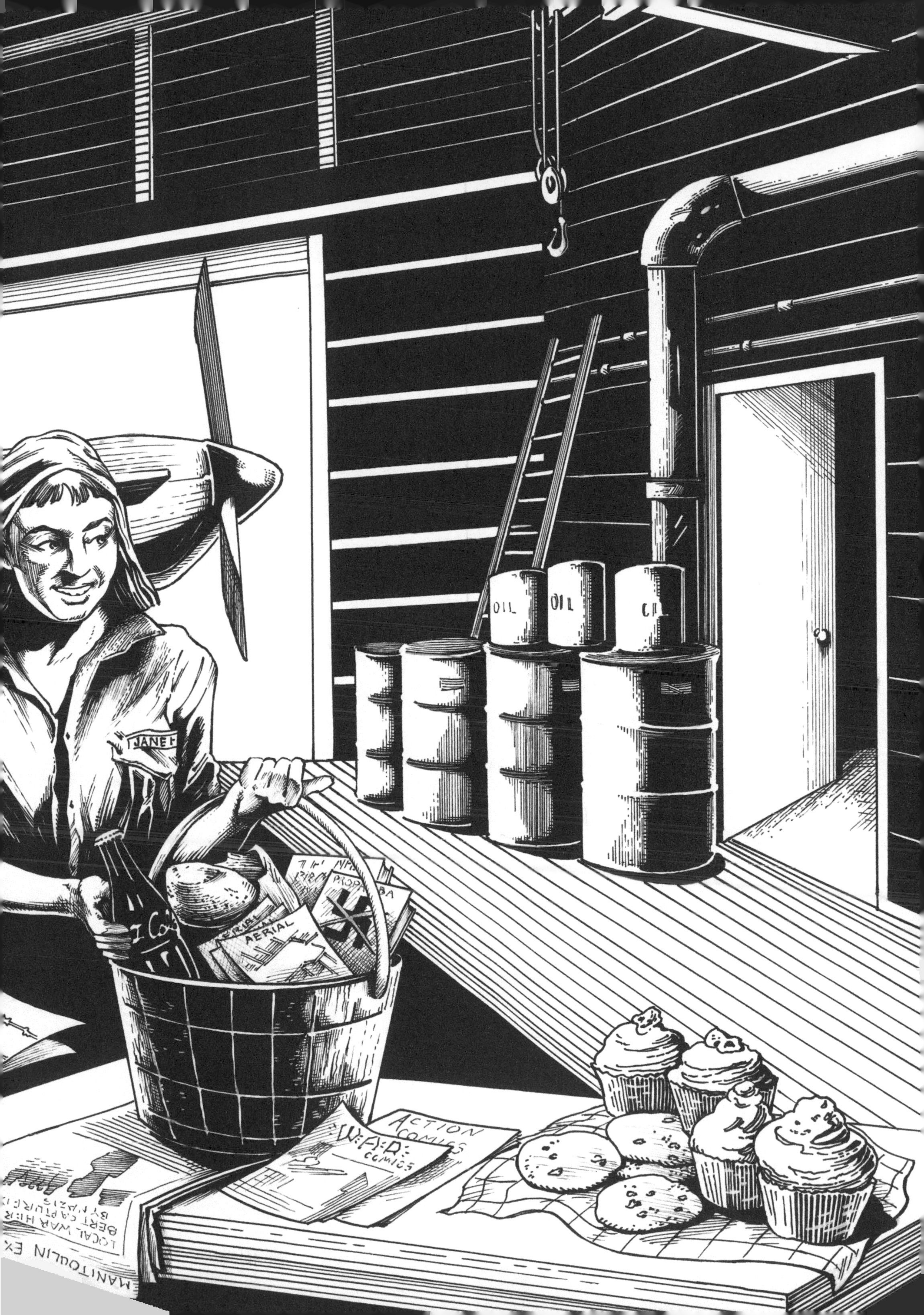
JANE H
OIL
OIL
AERIAL
ACTION COMICS

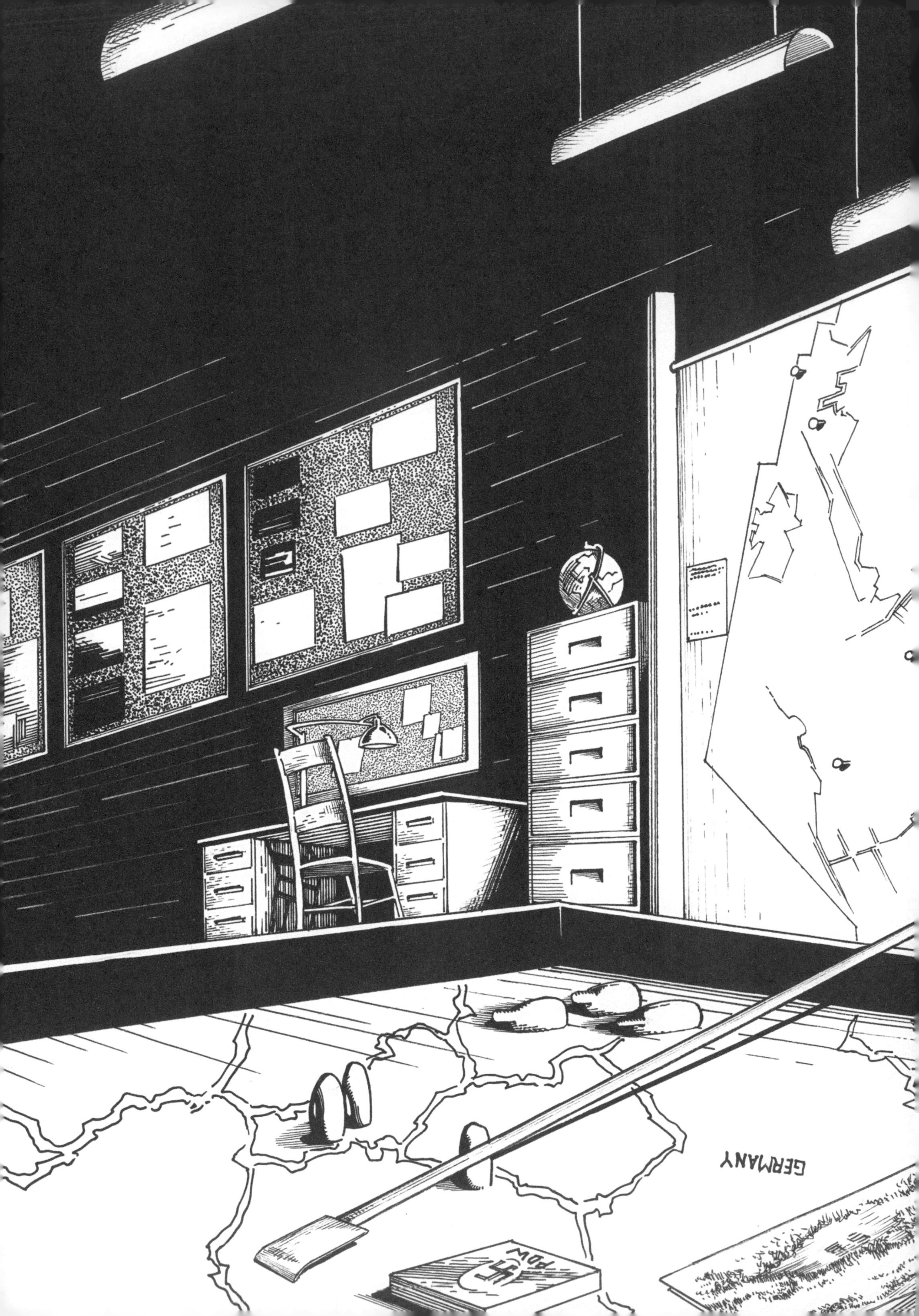
GERMANY
POW

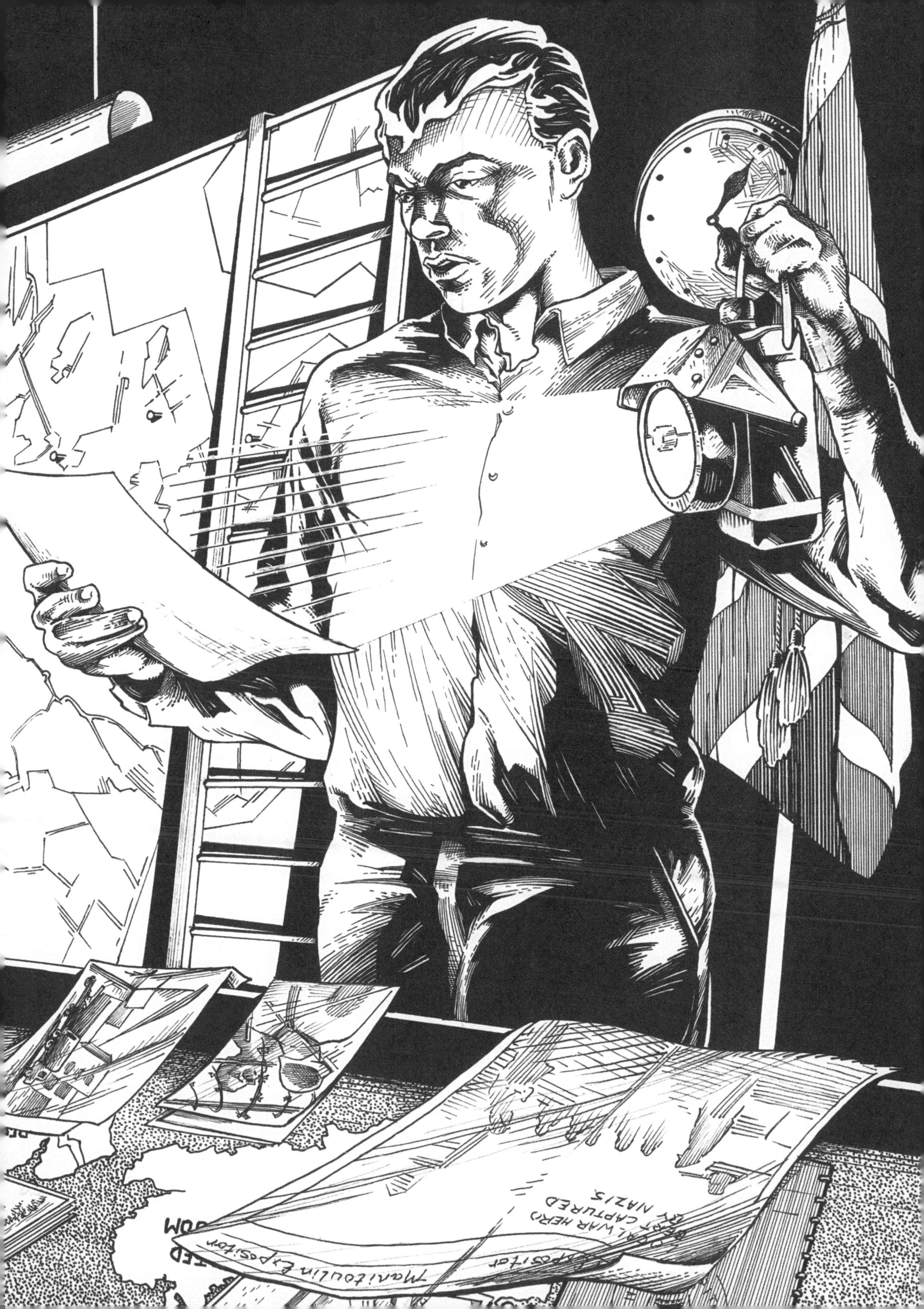

Manitoulin Expositor
CAPTURED
NAZIS

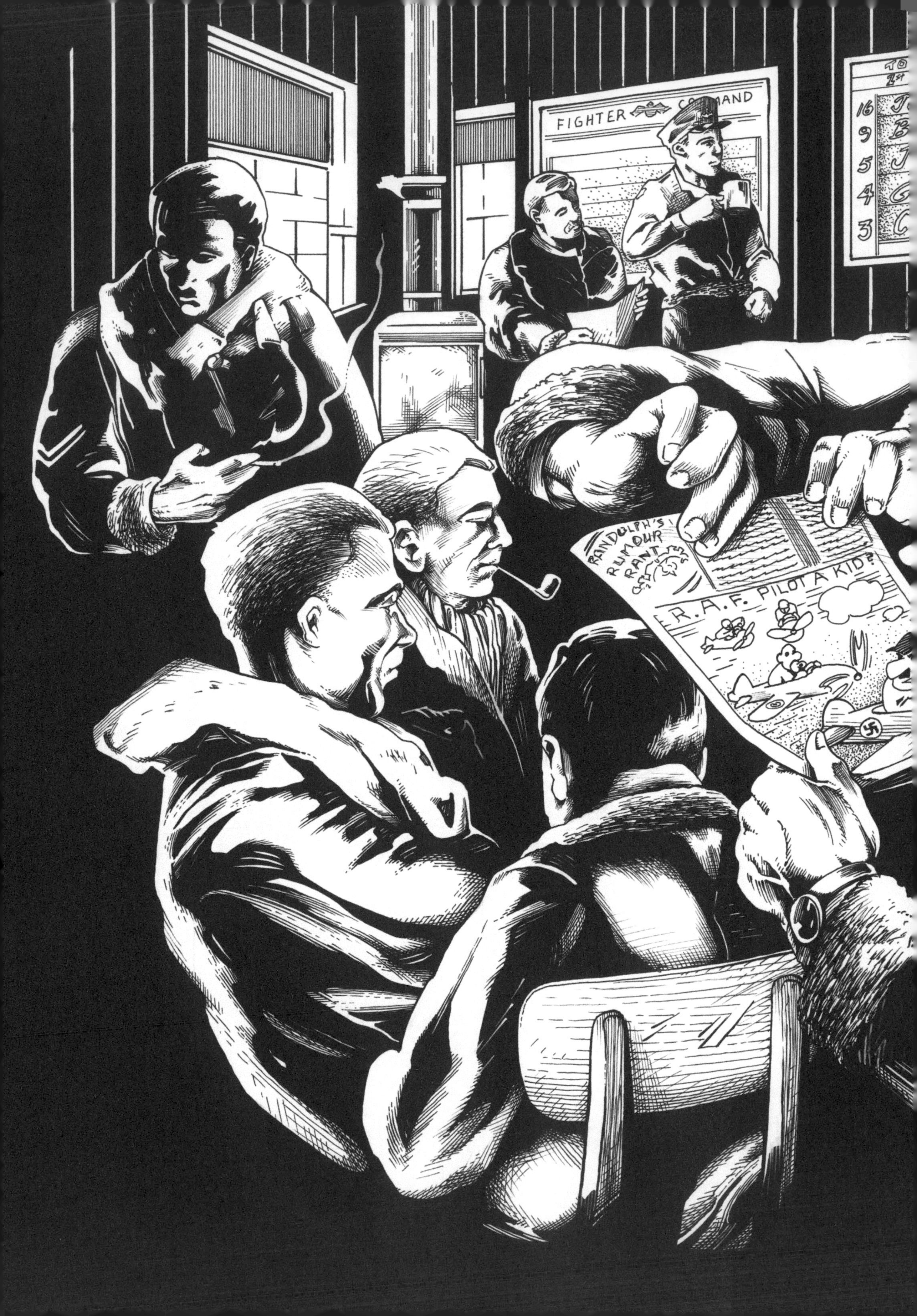
FIGHTER
RANDOLPH'S RUMOUR RANT
R.A.F. PILOT A KID?

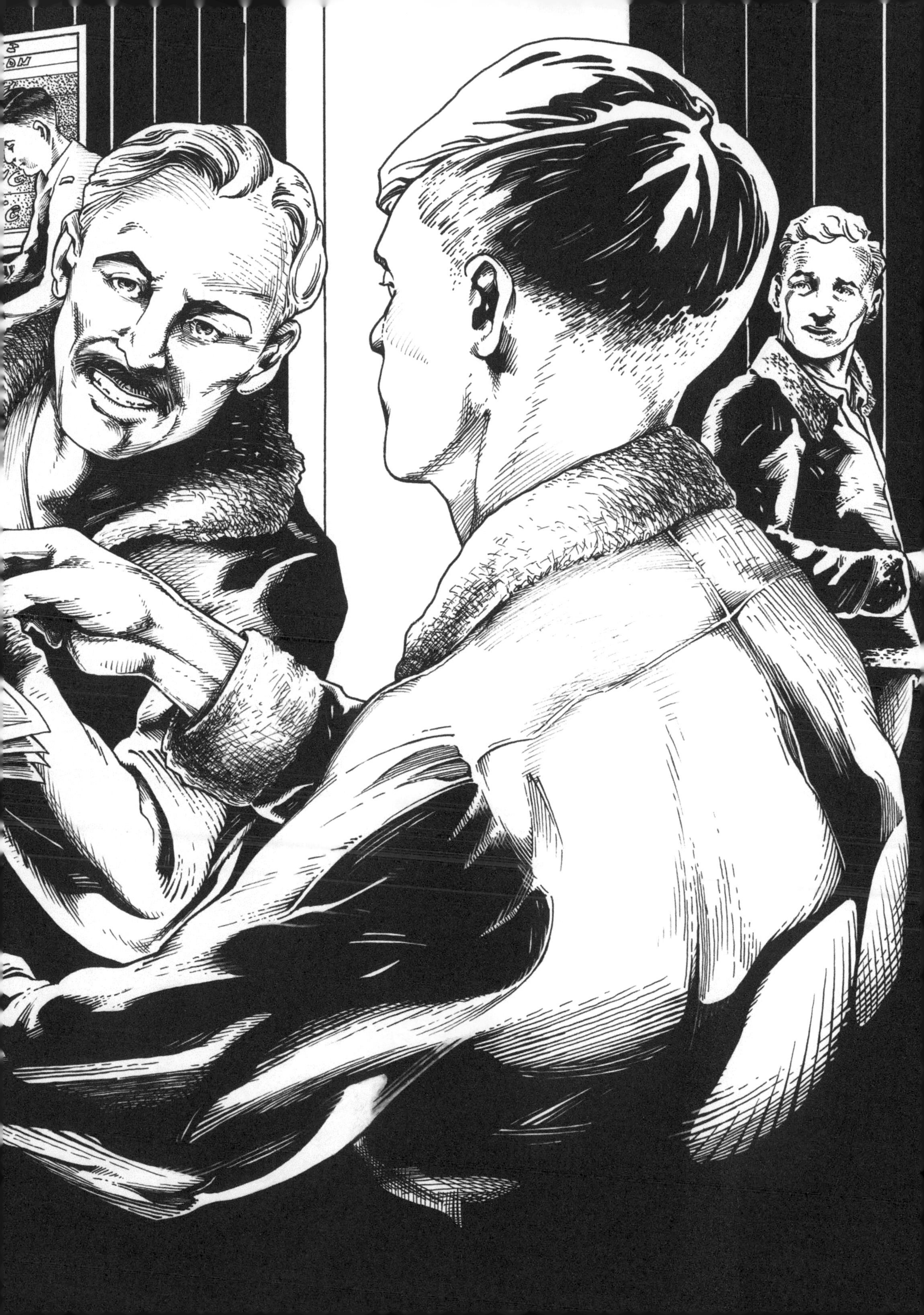

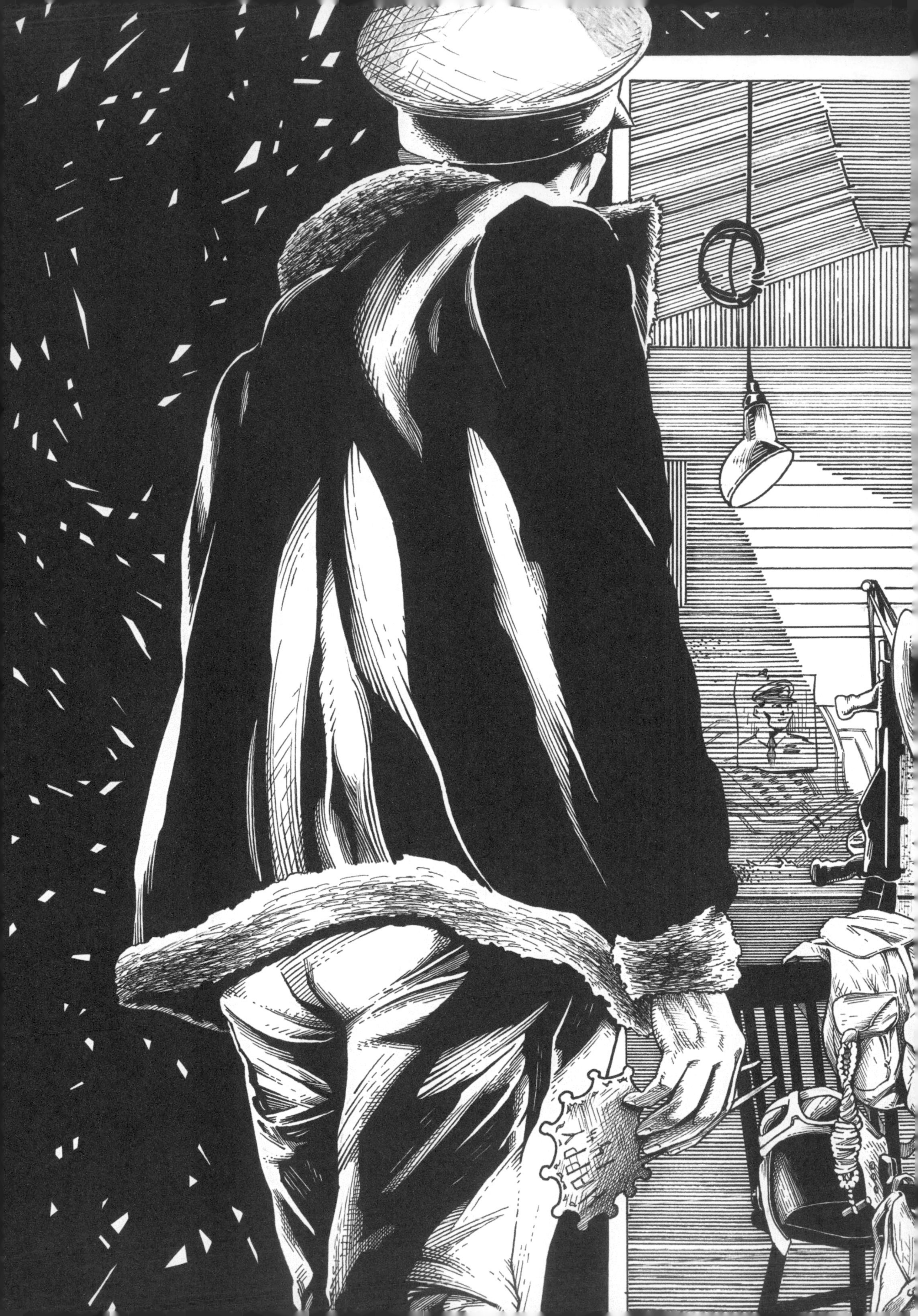

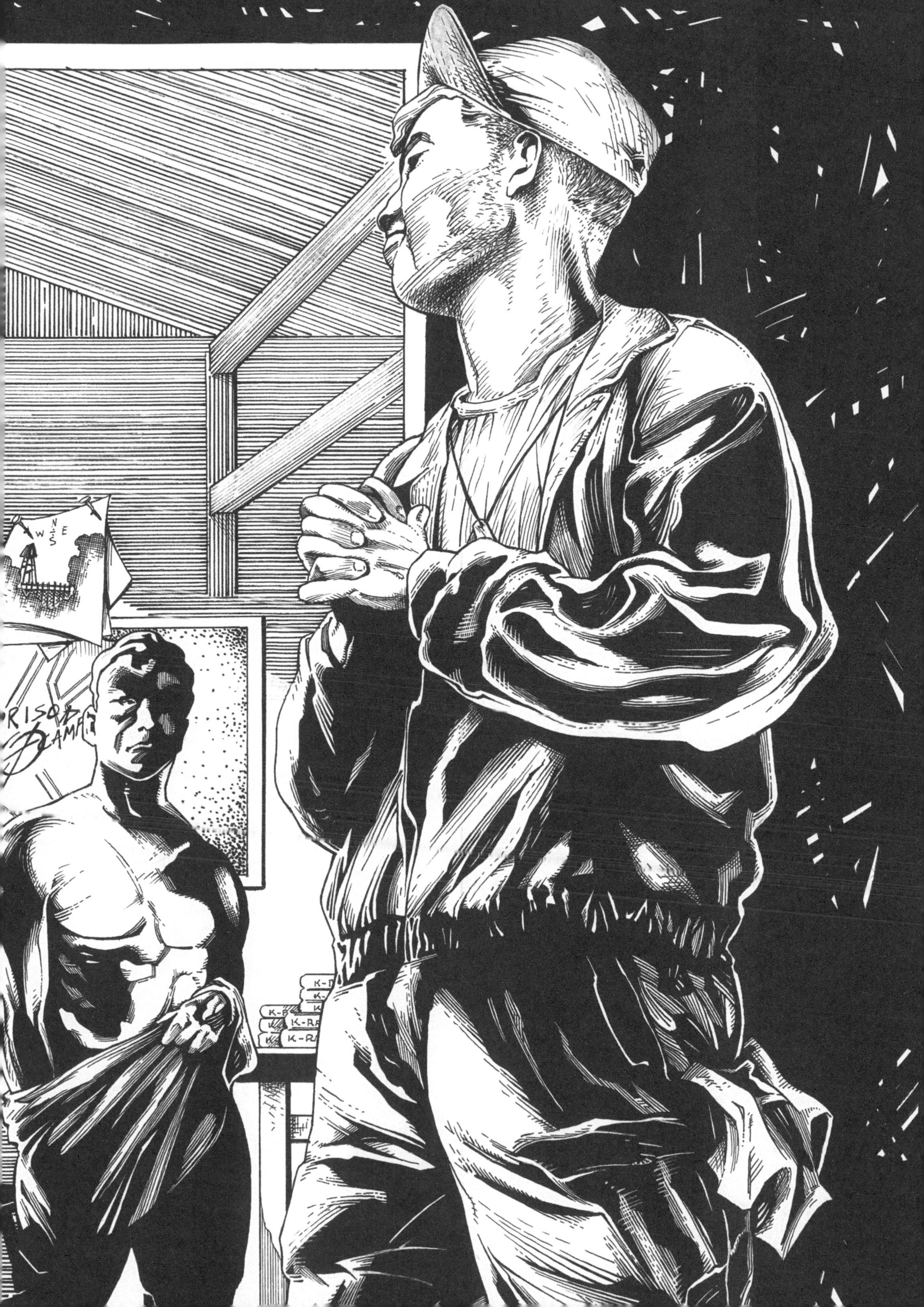

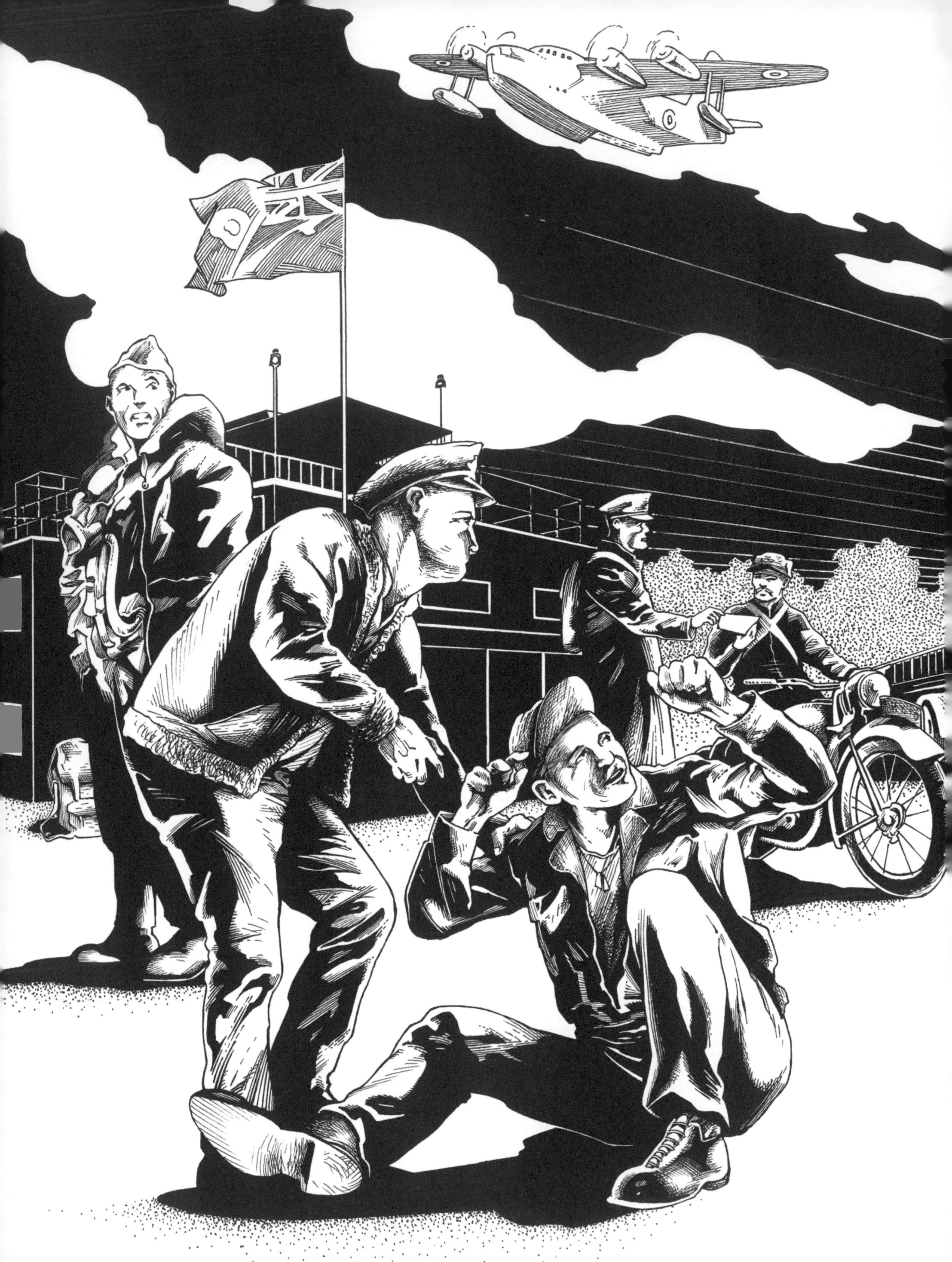

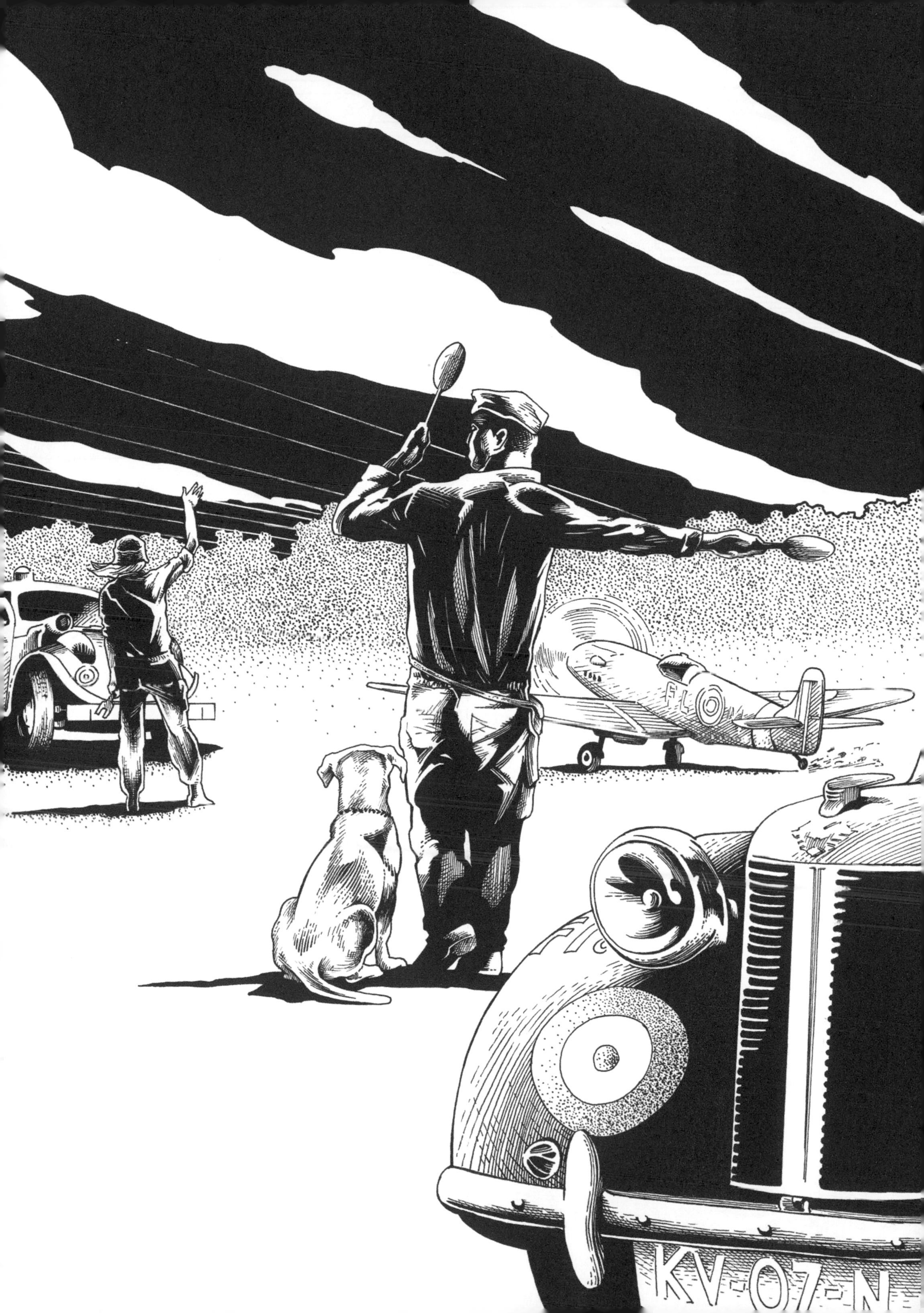
KV-07-N

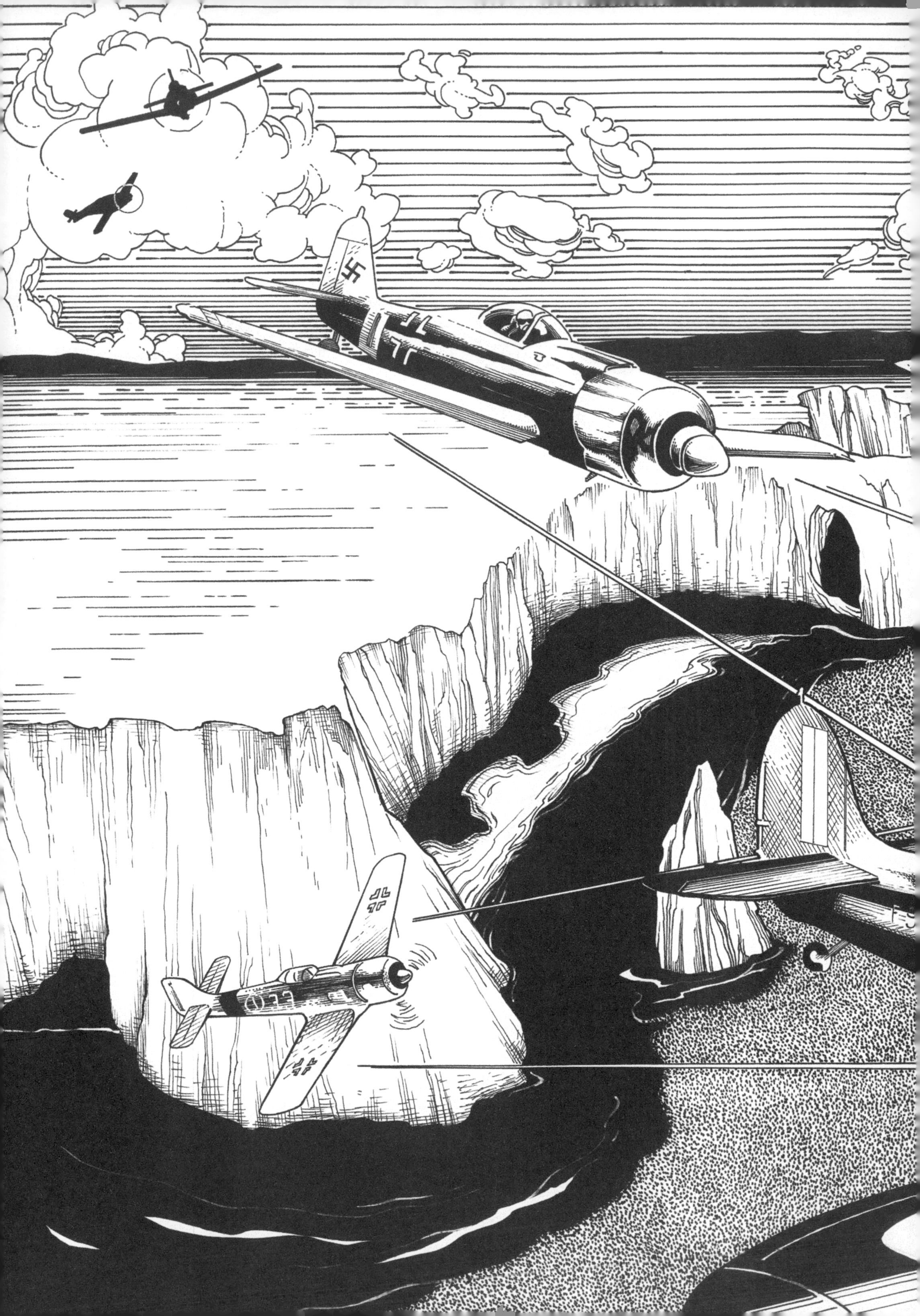

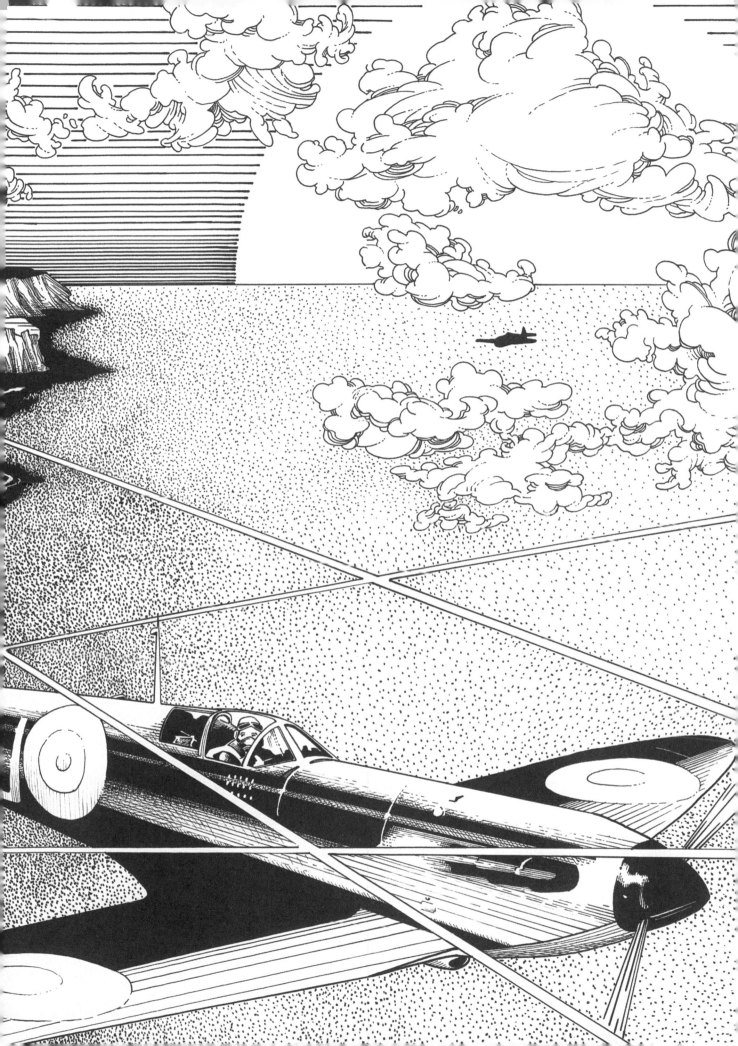

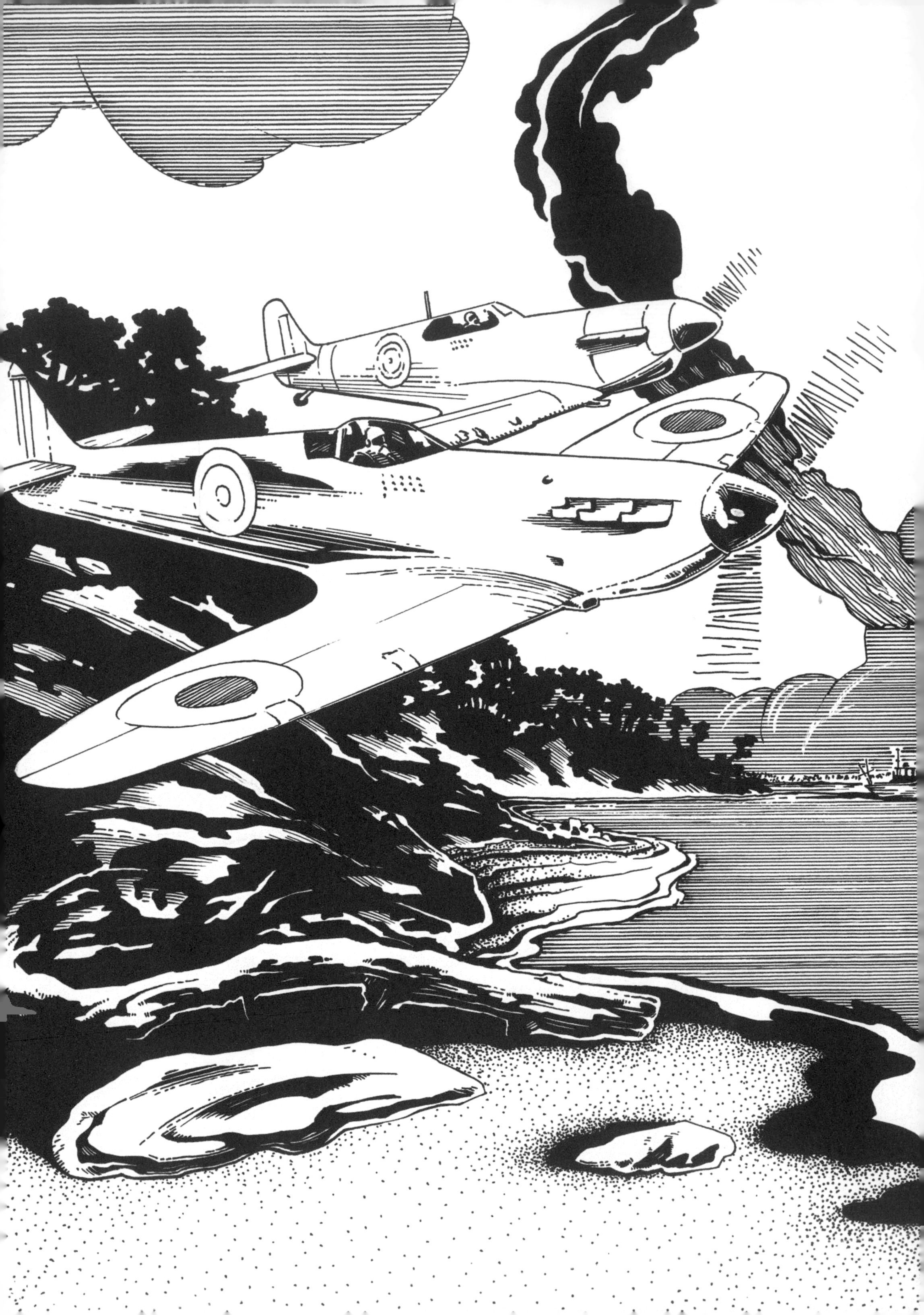

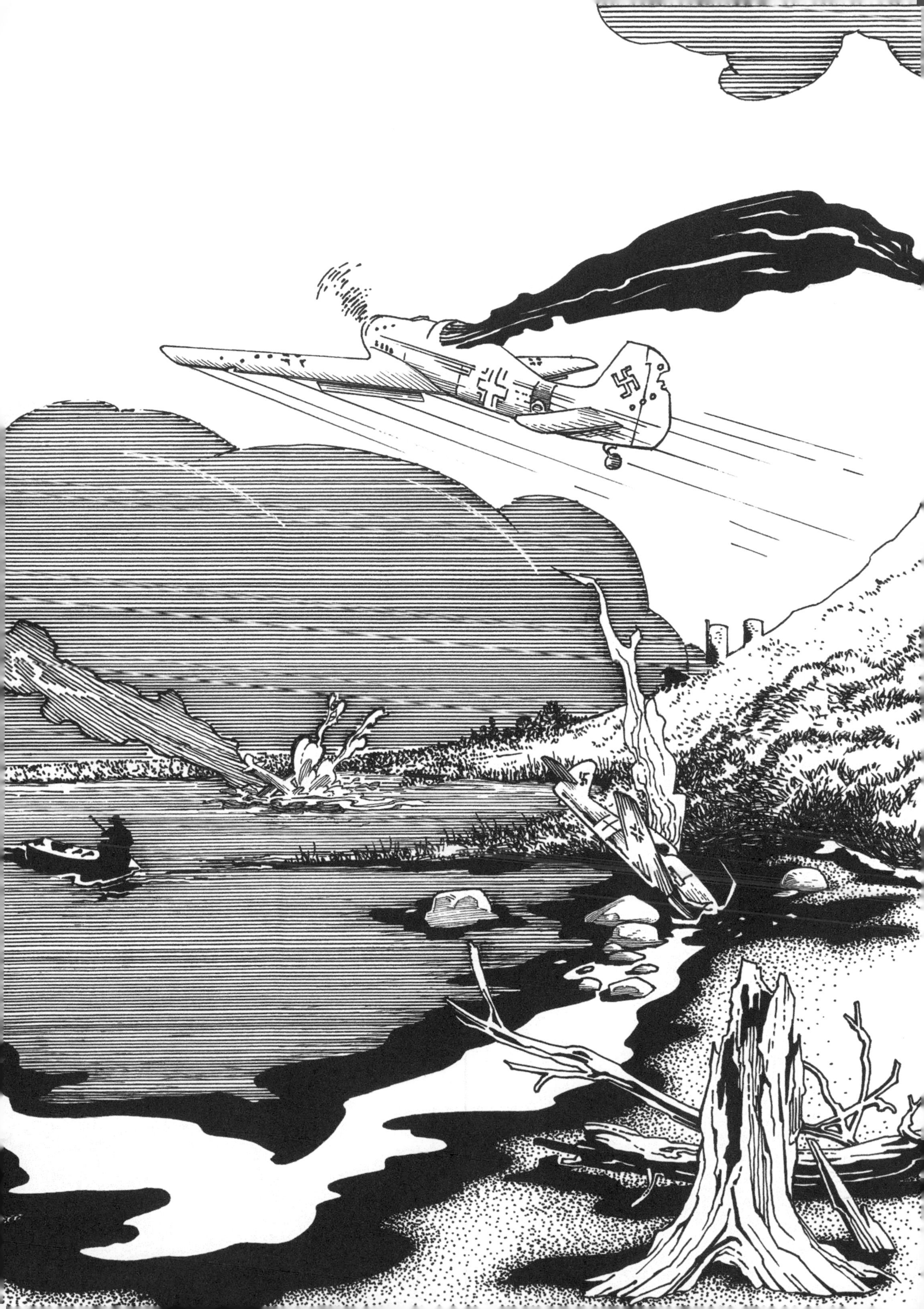

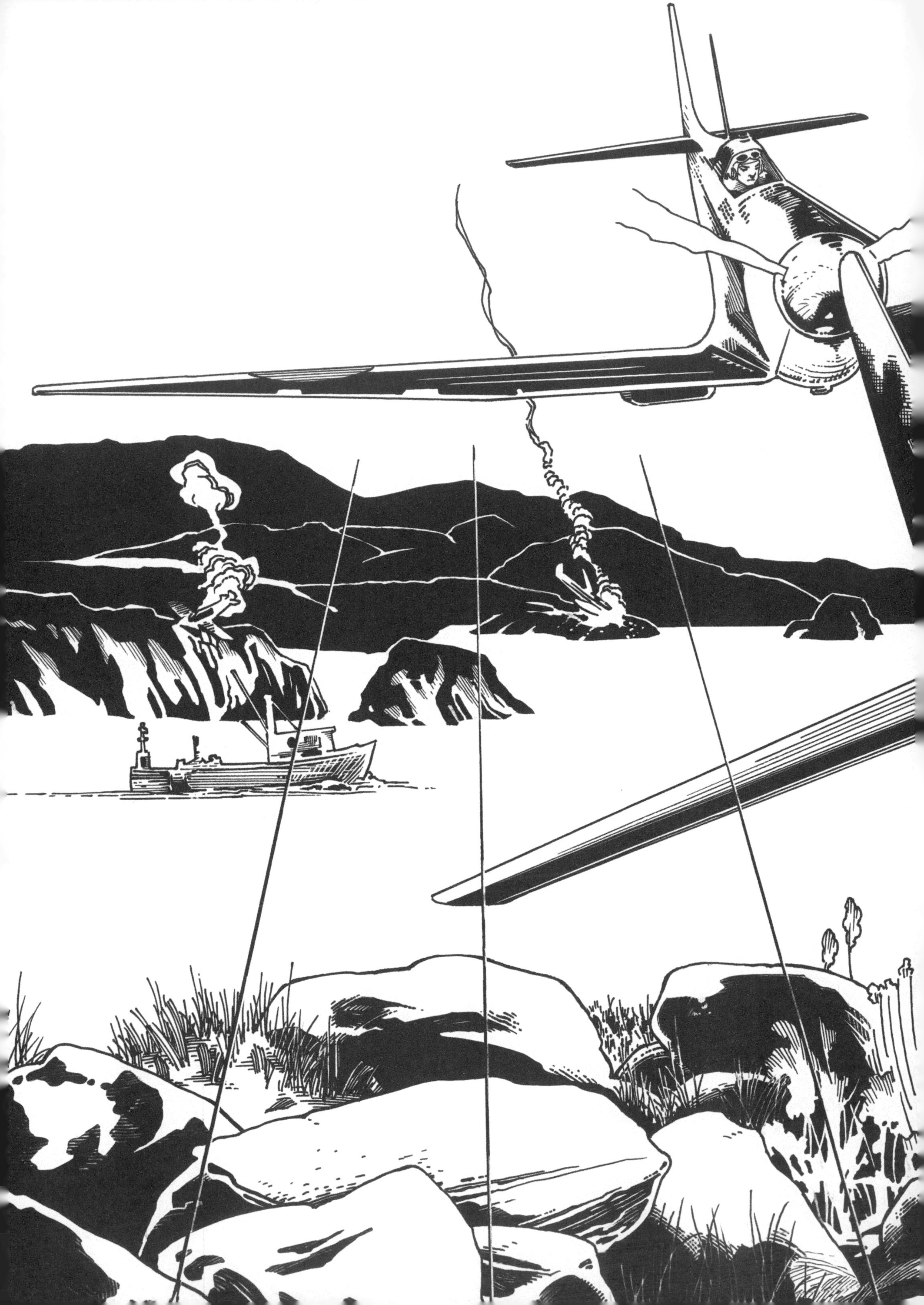

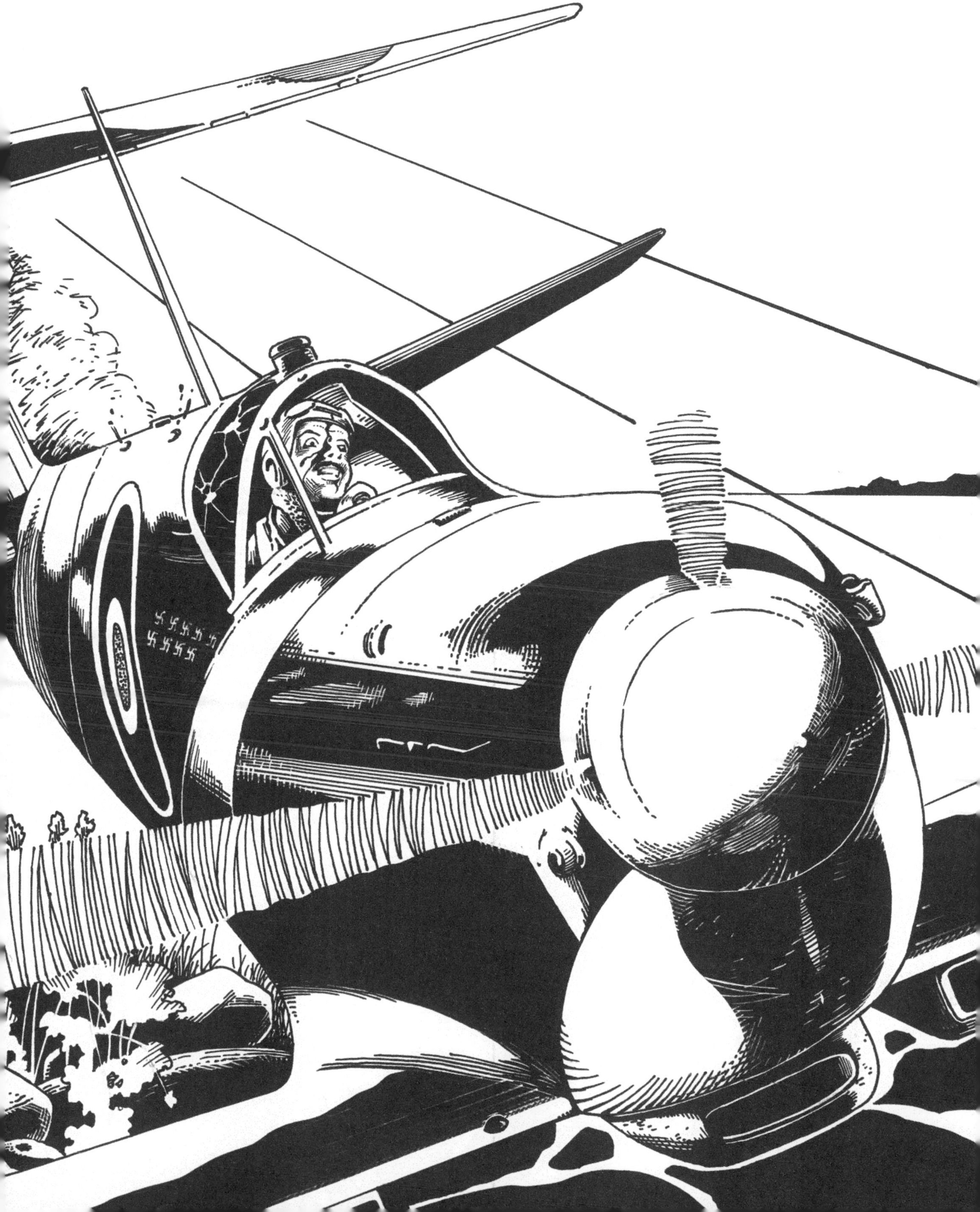

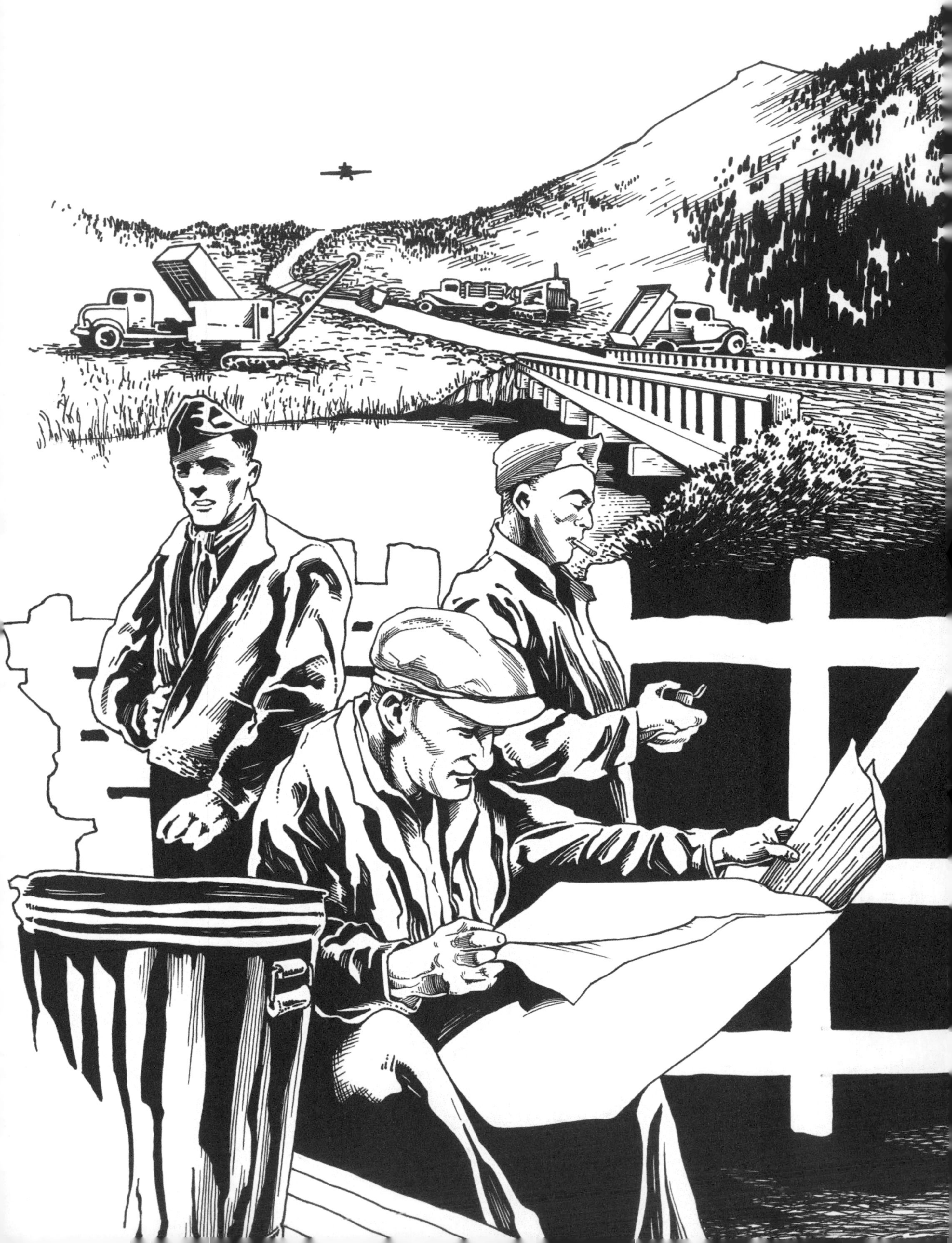

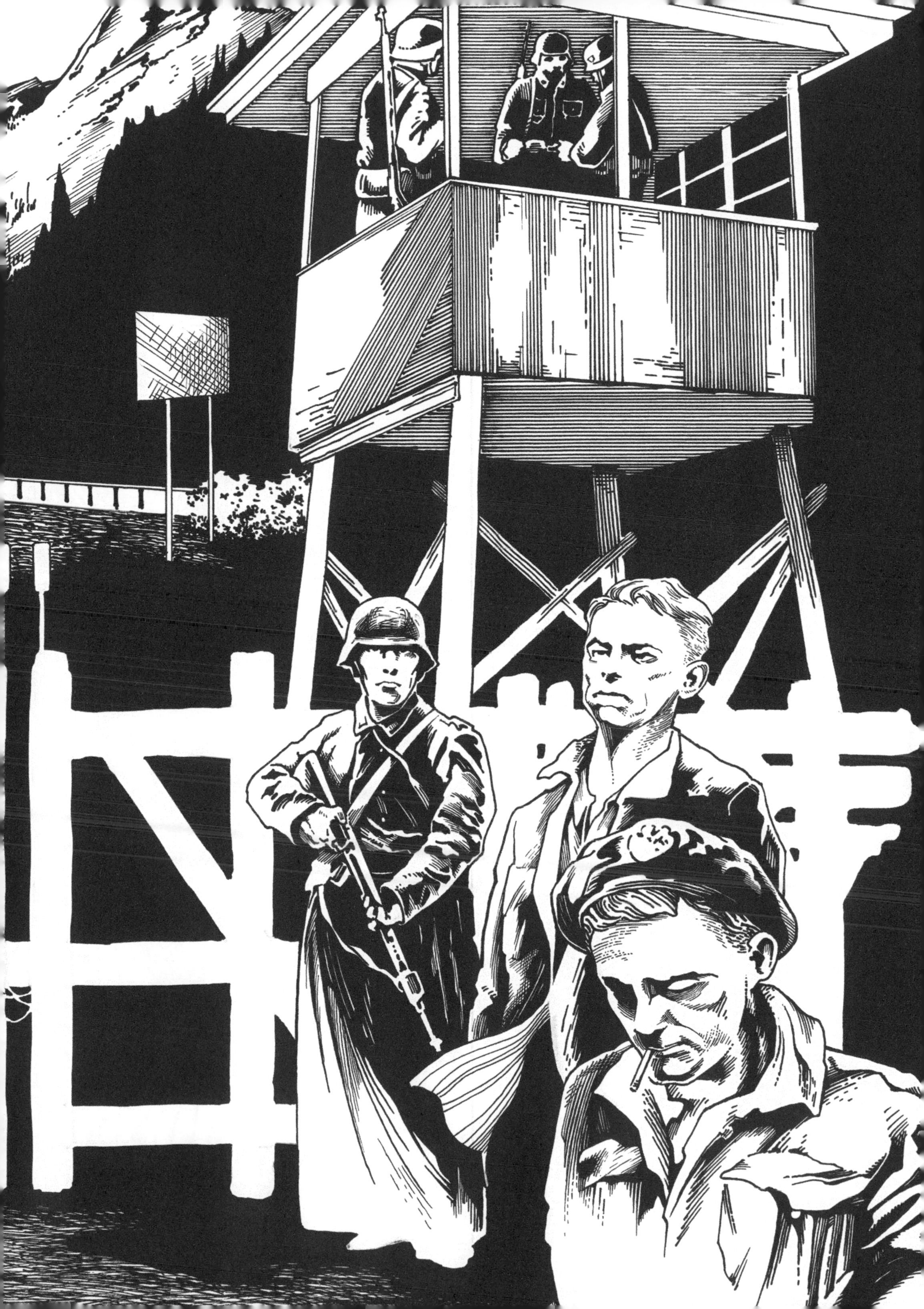

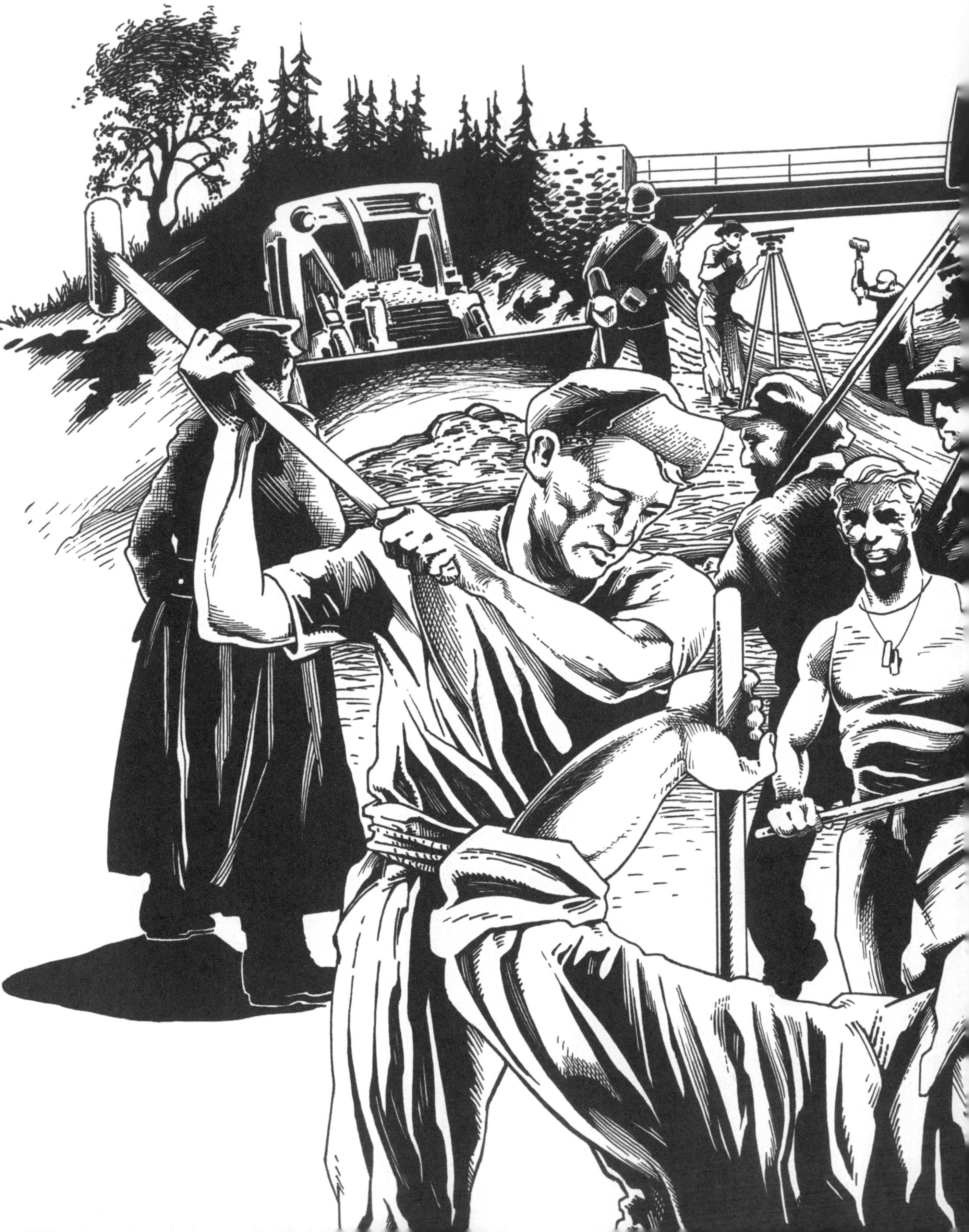

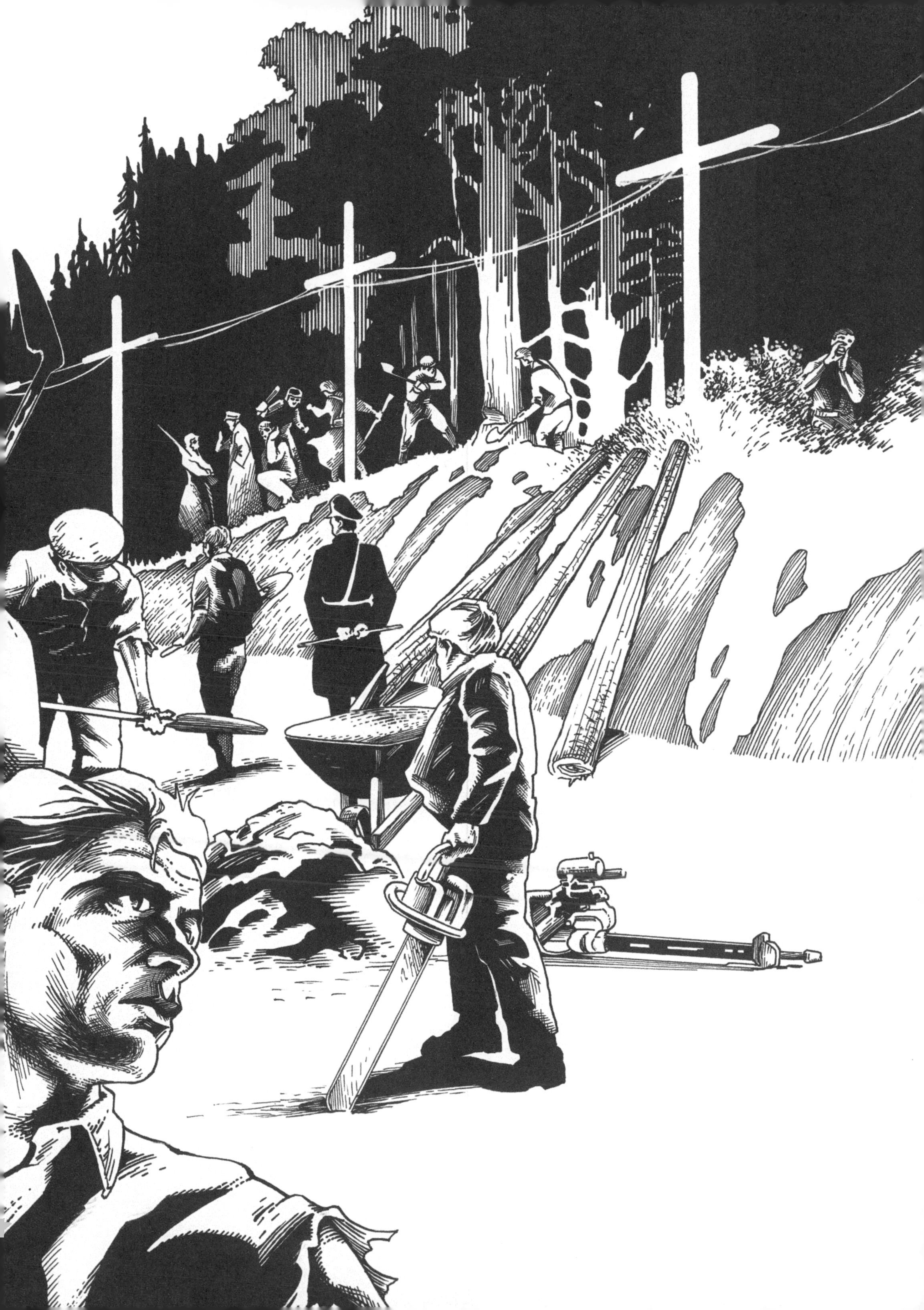

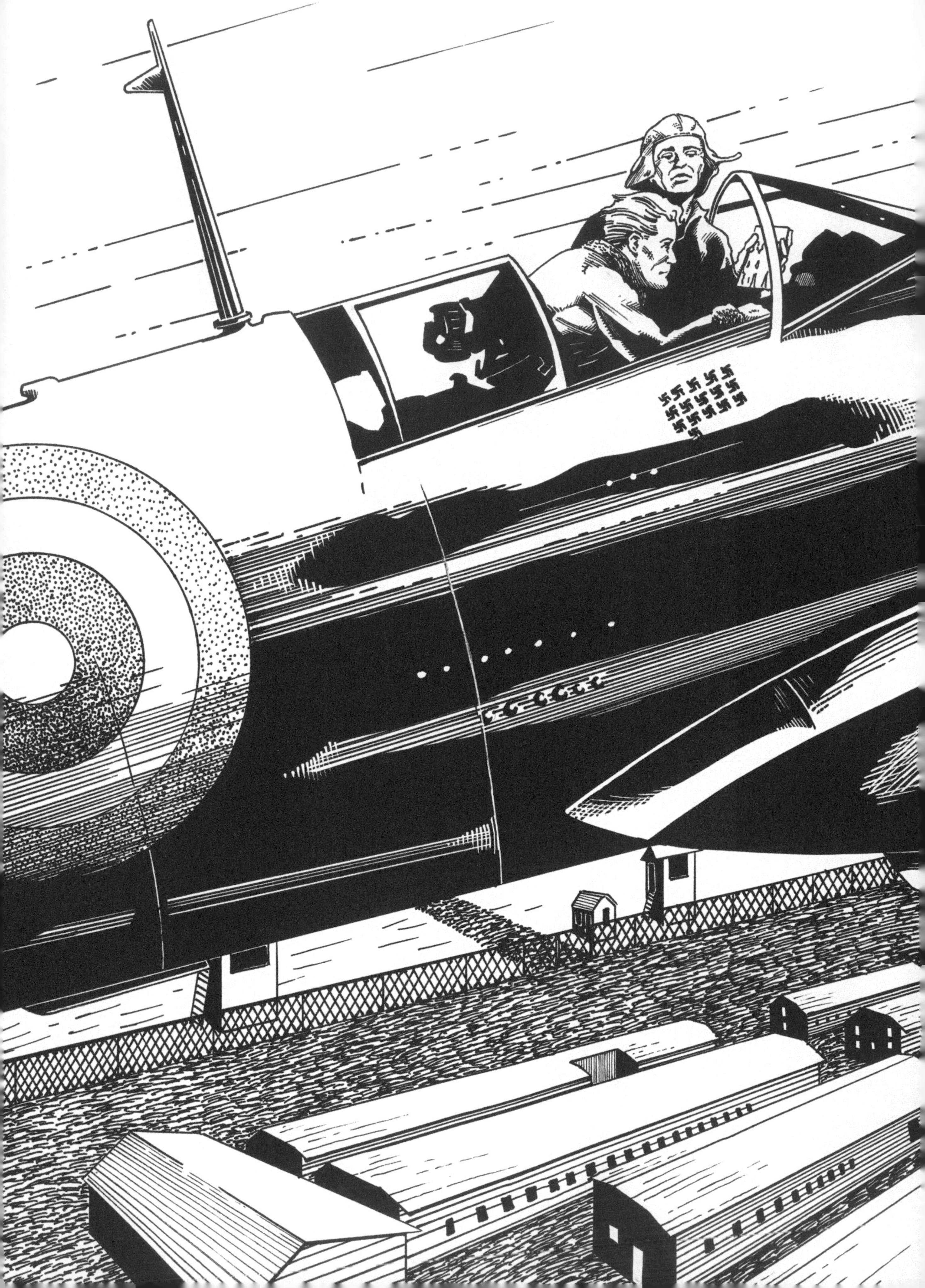

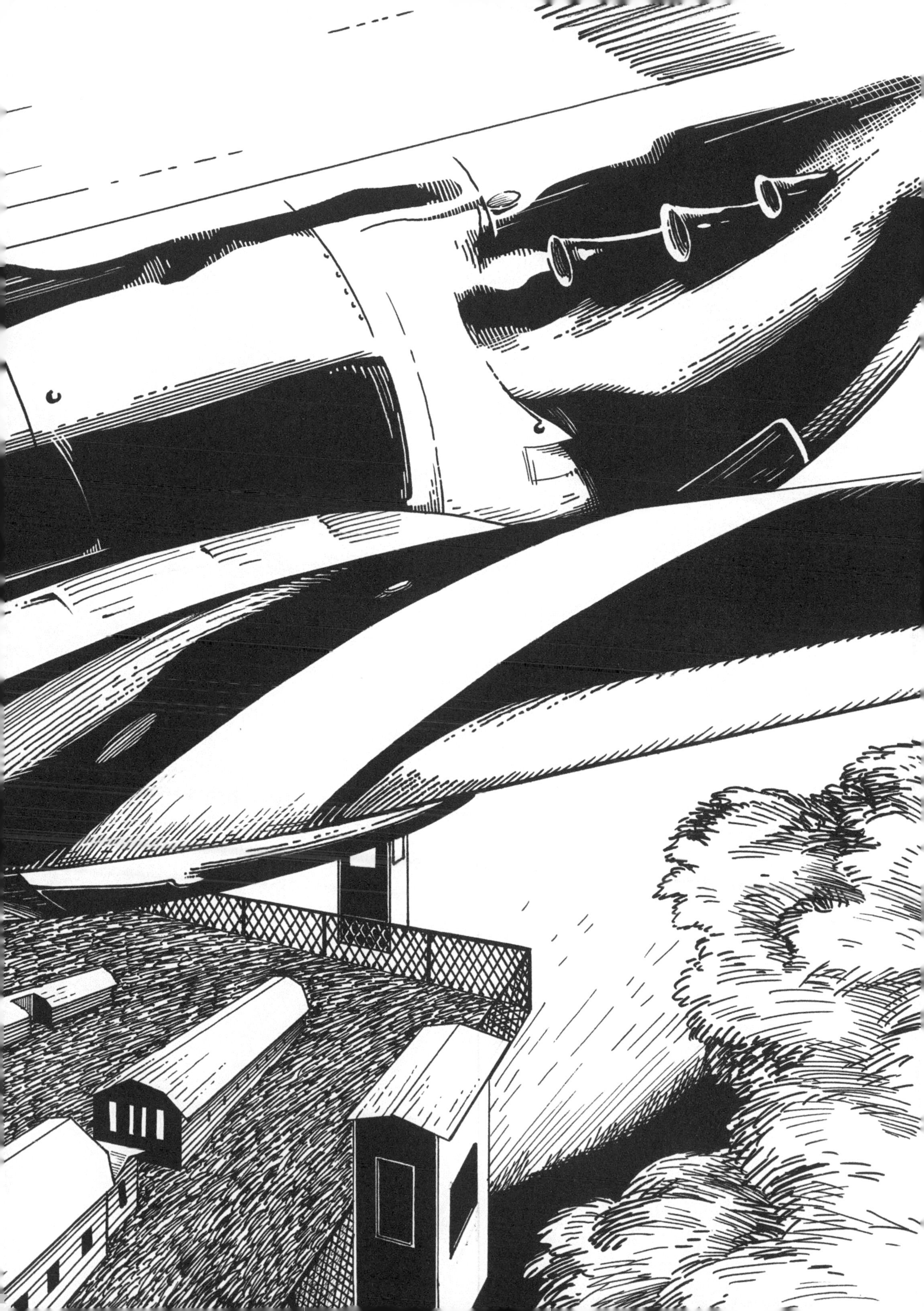

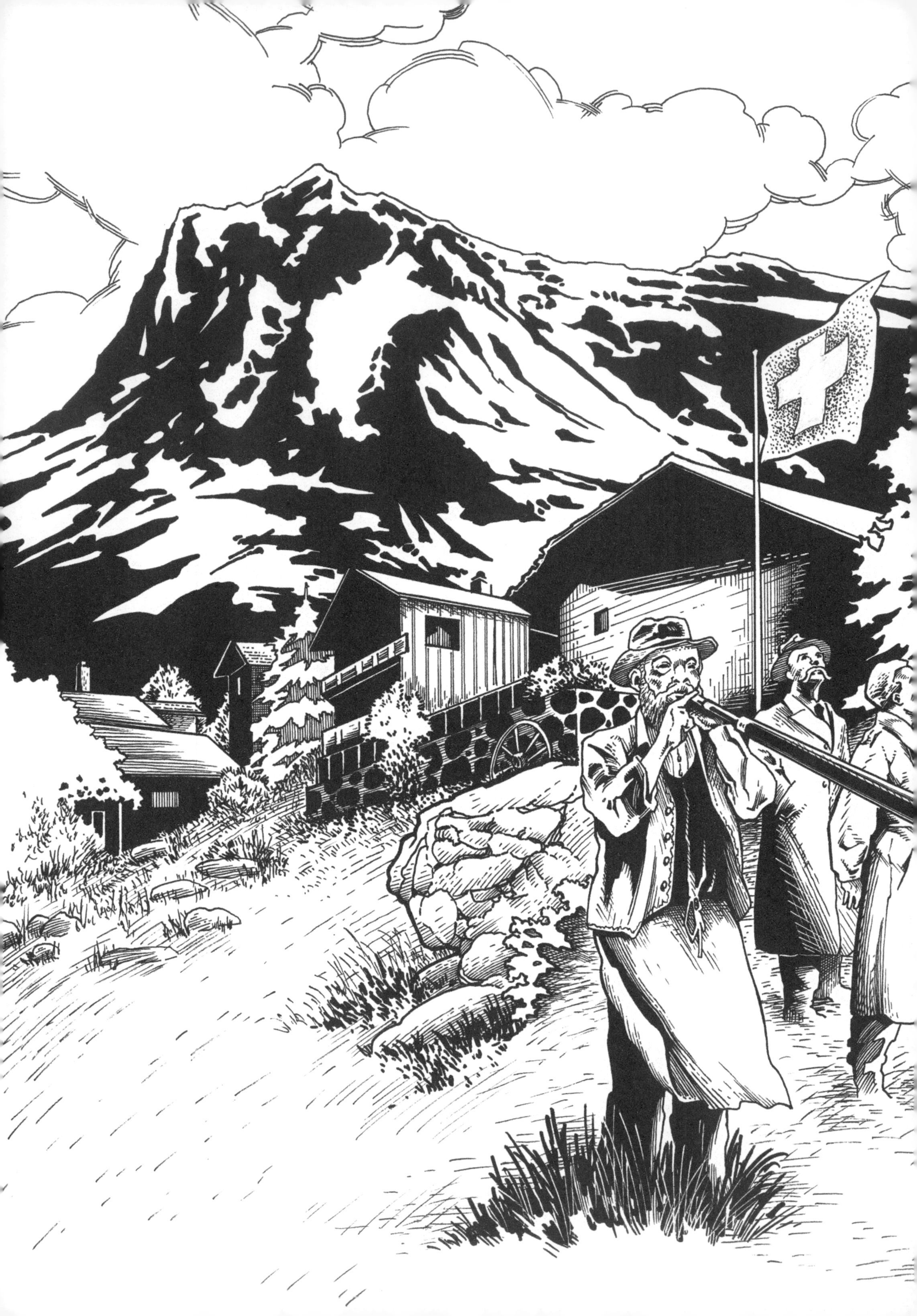

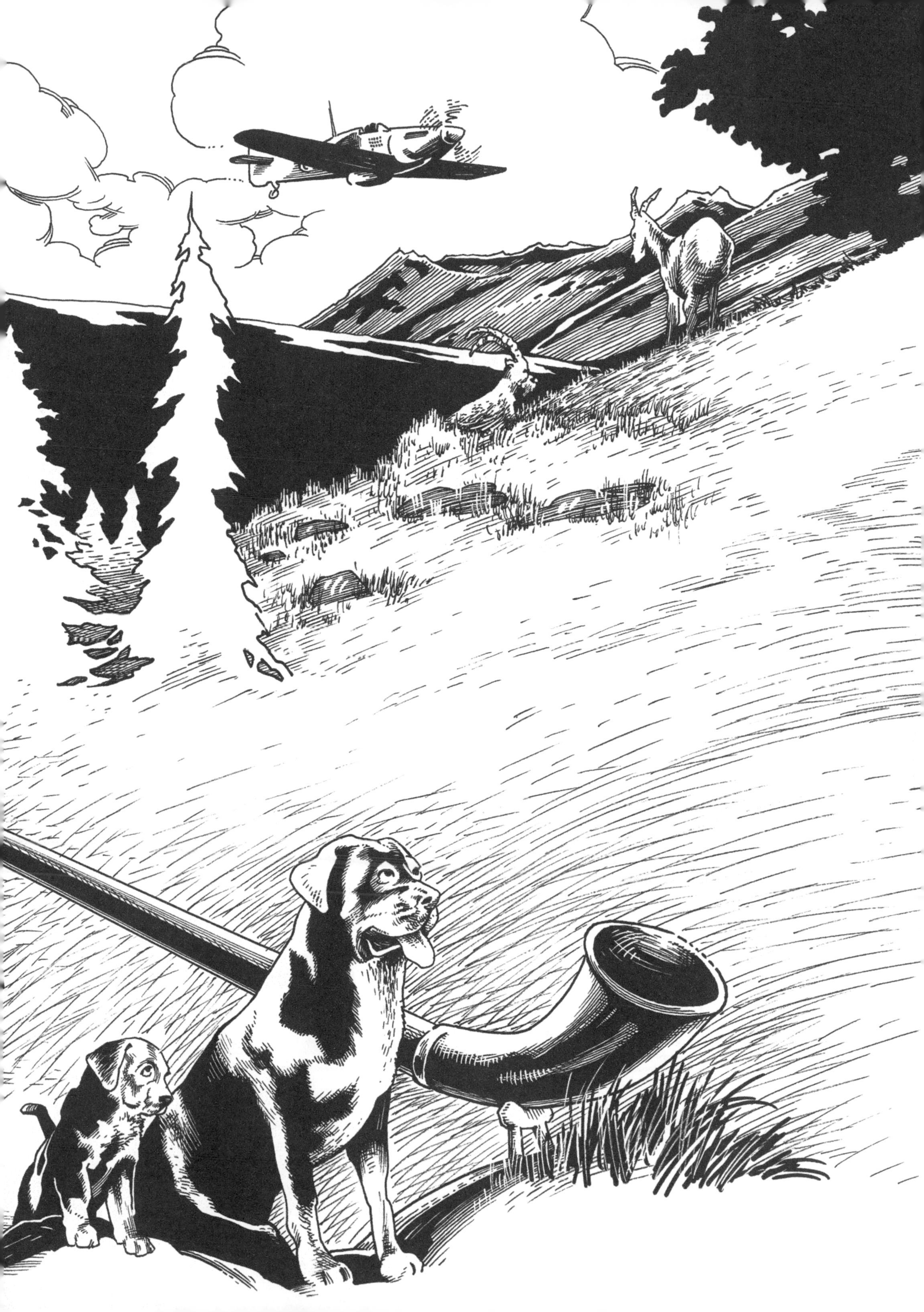

Theo Behe, Writer

Theo is a 14-year-old Canadian / British student at Highgate School. He loves playing football, novels, history, biology class and video games. Theo lives in a church in London, England and spends every summer on the lakes around North Bay, Canada. He is Markosia's youngest ever published comic writer. Theo had a great uncle named Bert who fought in World War Two.

Thomas Muzzell, Illustrator

Thomas is a 64-year-old Canadian professional comic artist. He has worked on hundreds of comics, books, movie storyboards and magazine features. Thomas lives in London, Canada right near his gym and two excellent comic book shops. Johnny Recruit is Thomas' 9th published comic book. Thomas had a great uncle named Bert who fought in World War Two.

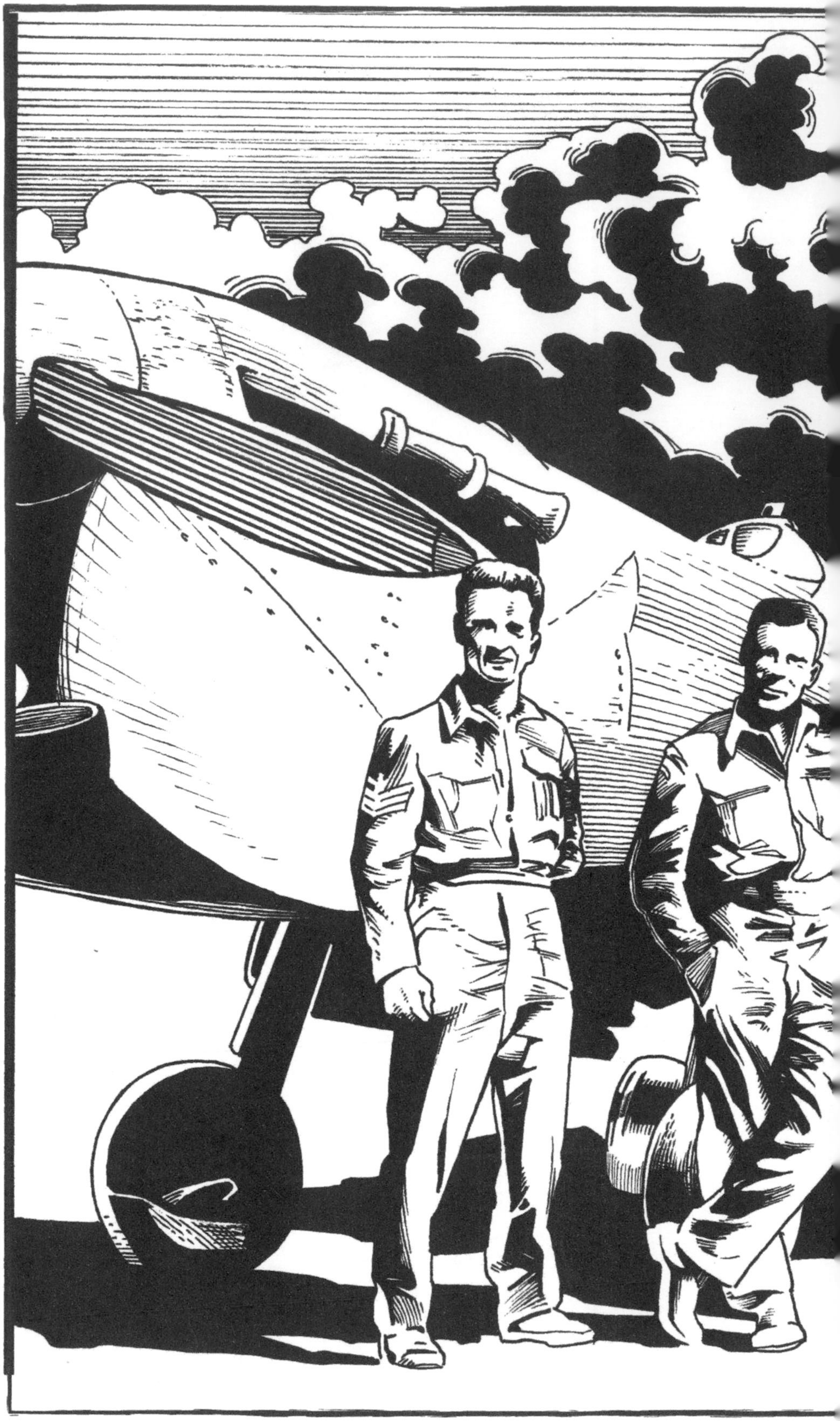

Albert "Bert" Houle, Inspiration

All-Canadian intercollegiate wrestling champion Bert joined the Royal Canadian Air Force in North Bay, Ontario and fought in North Africa, Malta and Italy.

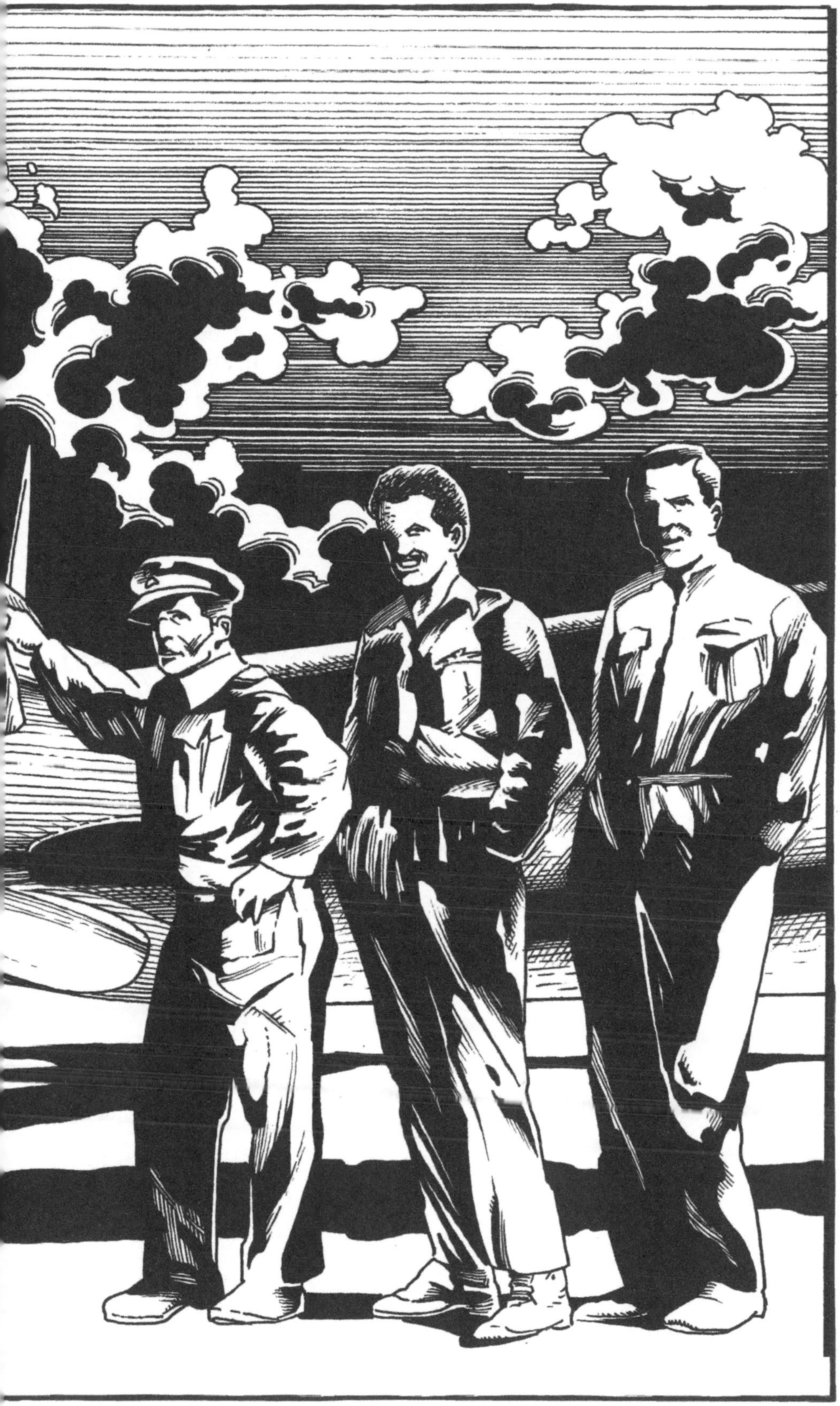

By 1942 he'd earned a Distinguished Flying Cross and two years later was awarded a Bar to his DFC by King George VI at Buckingham Palace. Bert achieved status of "double Ace" by downing 13½ enemy aircraft and died in 2008, aged 95.

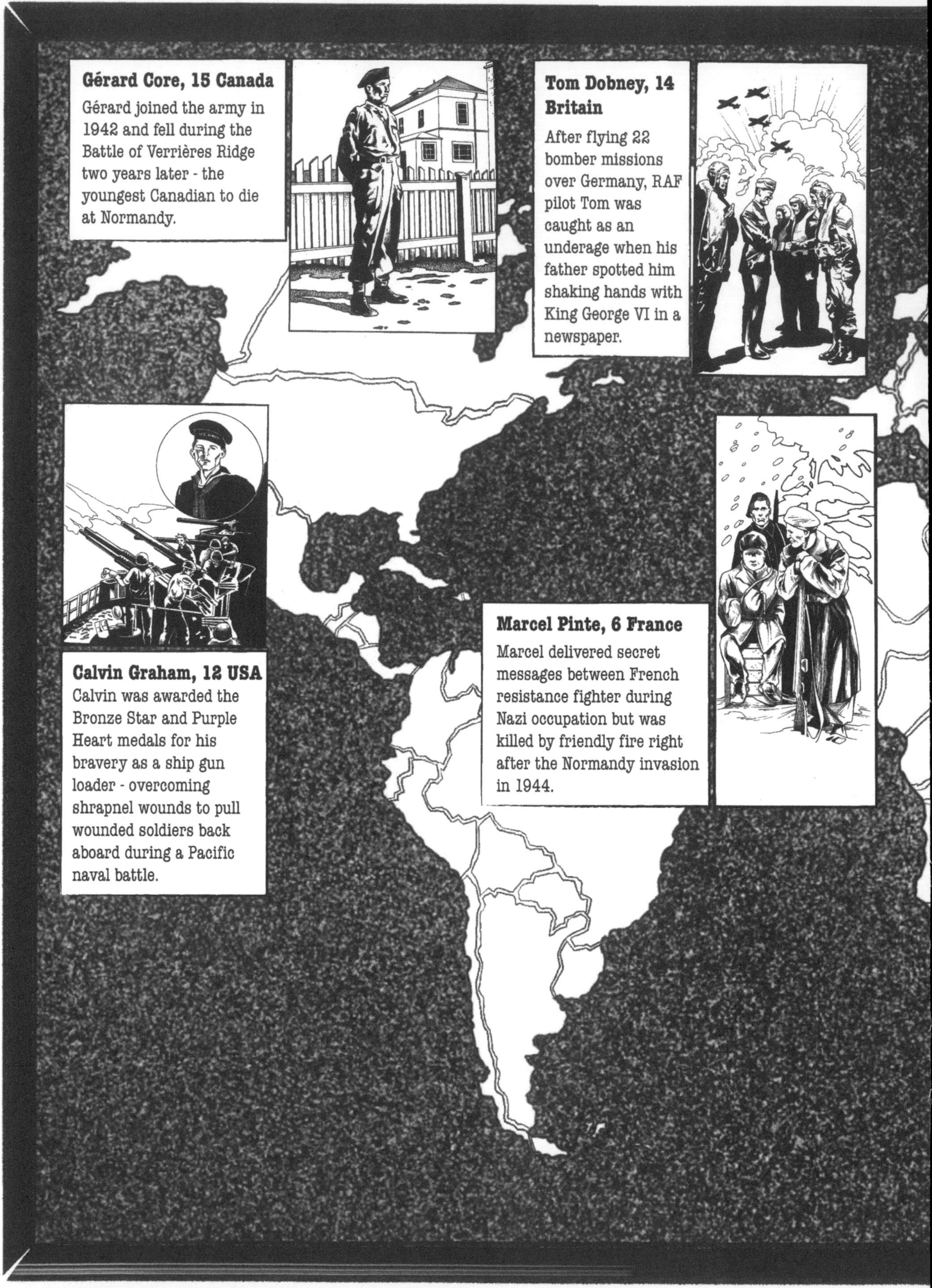
Gérard Core, 15 Canada
Gérard joined the army in 1942 and fell during the Battle of Verrières Ridge two years later - the youngest Canadian to die at Normandy.
Tom Dobney, 14 Britain
After flying 22 bomber missions over Germany, RAF pilot Tom was caught as an underage when his father spotted him shaking hands with King George VI in a newspaper.
Calvin Graham, 12 USA
Calvin was awarded the Bronze Star and Purple Heart medals for his bravery as a ship gun loader - overcoming shrapnel wounds to pull wounded soldiers back aboard during a Pacific naval battle.
Marcel Pinte, 6 France
Marcel delivered secret messages between French resistance fighter during Nazi occupation but was killed by friendly fire right after the Normandy invasion in 1944.

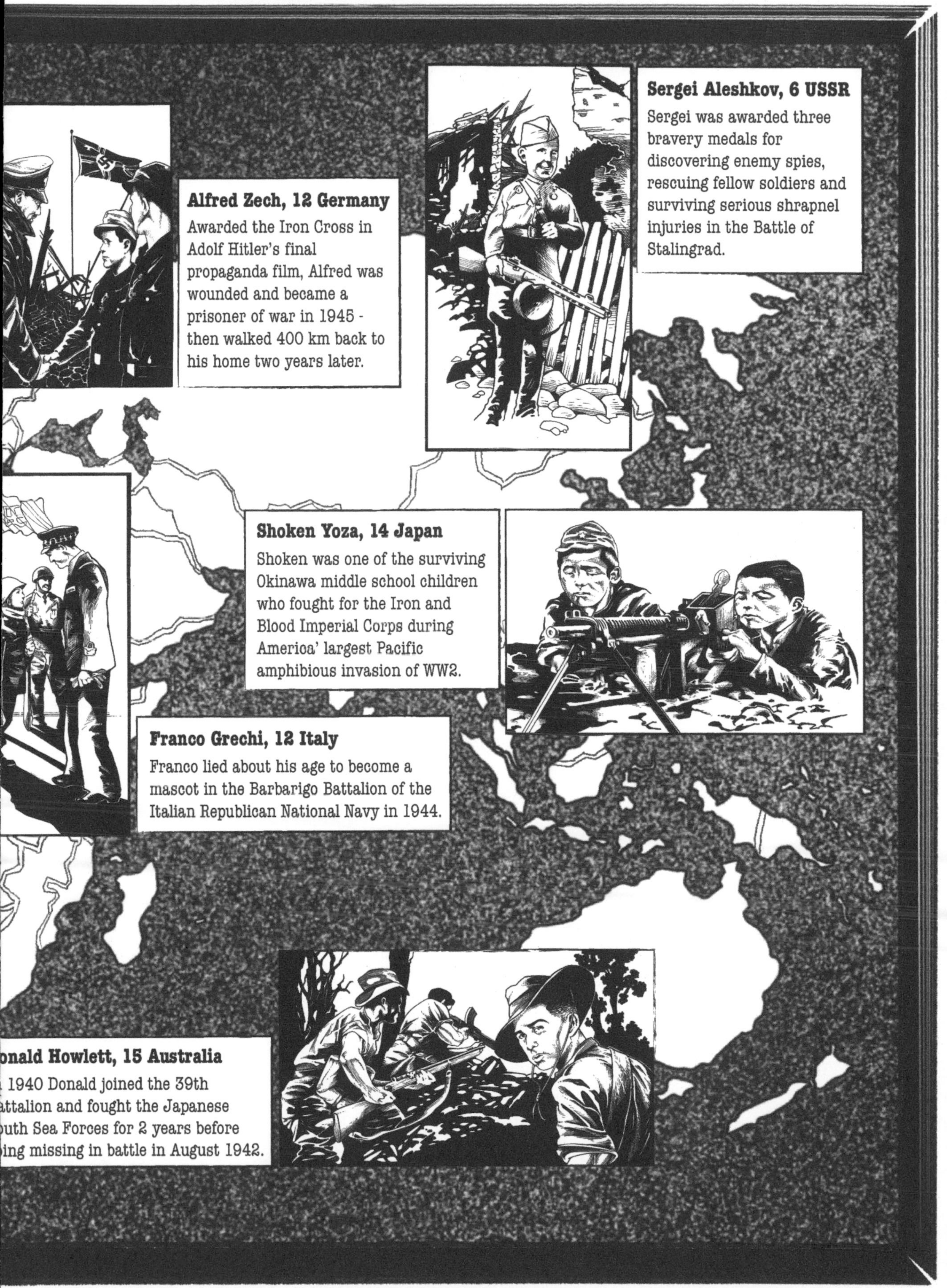
Sergei Aleshkov, 6 USSR
Sergei was awarded three bravery medals for discovering enemy spies, rescuing fellow soldiers and surviving serious shrapnel injuries in the Battle of Stalingrad.
Alfred Zech, 12 Germany
Awarded the Iron Cross in Adolf Hitler's final propaganda film, Alfred was wounded and became a prisoner of war in 1945 - then walked 400 km back to his home two years later.
Shoken Yoza, 14 Japan
Shoken was one of the surviving Okinawa middle school children who fought for the Iron and Blood Imperial Corps during America' largest Pacific amphibious invasion of WW2.
Franco Grechi, 12 Italy
Franco lied about his age to become a mascot in the Barbarigo Battalion of the Italian Republican National Navy in 1944.
onald Howlett, 15 Australia
1940 Donald joined the 39th attalion and fought the Japanese outh Sea Forces for 2 years before oing missing in battle in August 1942.

JOHNNY RECRUIT

www.contrabandgraphicnovel.com/johnnyrecruit
facebook.com/johnnyrecruit
tjbehe@gmail.com

MARKOSIA

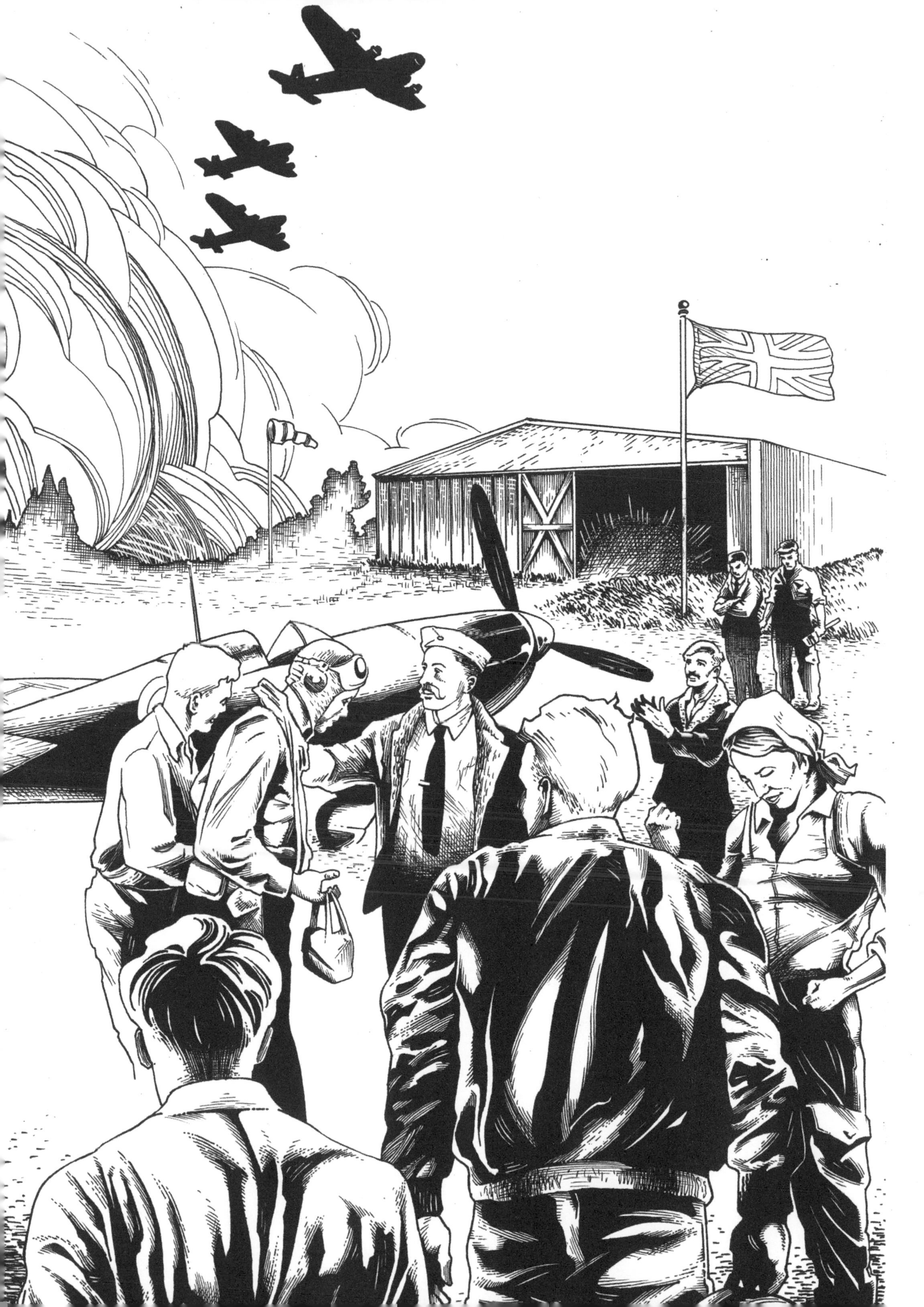

www.markosia.com

Lightning Source UK Ltd.
Milton Keynes UK
UKHW051711170522
403080UK00002BA/132